D1025123

LIFE IN BRITAIN
BETWEEN THE WARS

Life in Britain
BETWEEN
THE WARS

L.C.B. SEAMAN

English Life Series
EDITED BY PETER QUENNELL

LONDON: B. T. Batsford Ltd
NEW YORK: G. P. Putnam's Sons

First published 1970

© L. C. B. Seaman, 1970

7134 1462 6

Made and printed in Great Britain
by Jarrold & Sons Ltd, Norwich
for the publishers
B. T. BATSFORD LTD
4 Fitzhardinge Street, London W.1
G. P. PUTNAM'S SONS
200 Madison Avenue, New York, NY 10016

Preface

This survey of English life between the wars is the product of much study of the period, both during it and afterwards. One who writes as an eyewitness is perhaps prone to accord to personal reminiscence an often spurious general validity; nevertheless, I have felt compelled on certain topics to ignore much that previous writers, academic or otherwise, have said about the period, and to include other material for which, as yet, no serious historical study exists.

Much has been omitted. This is in part because the book seeks to concentrate on matters that were significant for the times and for large numbers of people. Thus, although the 'intrepid aviators' of those years did much to increase the sales of newspapers, the first real significance of the flying-machine for most people was its use in war as a device for trying to kill them. Similarly, almost nothing is said of those scientific and technological discoveries (from the geiger counter to the cyclotron, radar and the first jet-engine) whose significance lay wholly in the future. Nor have the major intellectual and artistic achievements of the time been more than touched on; and this is because, perhaps, the first requisites for a sympathetic approach to the interwar years are a willingness to risk being accused of philistinism and an ability not to be shocked at the first signs of an emergent mass culture.

No one attempting in so small a compass to deal with many diverse aspects of life can escape falling into error on the way. While absolving them for any responsibility for the fallibility of what follows, I would thank my friends and colleagues, Messrs J. B. Watson and Alan Pearson, for their help on a number of details ranging from the northern music-halls to the mysteries of League and County cricket, and G. J. Talbot for his help at the proof stage; Mr Trevor Millum, without whose help I would have failed to do justice to women's magazines; and my son John, who compelled me to look more thoughtfully than I might otherwise have done at the design, domestic and architectural, of the time. I have also to thank my wife for her harrowing tales of life in a girls' school, her guidance on matters of women's dress, her general forbearance, and her willingness, in the cause of this book, to deny herself the services of one of the deftest manual dishwashers in the kingdom.

Woking 1970   L.C.B.S.

Contents

Acknowledgment

The author and publisher wish to thank the following for permission to quote from the books listed below (page references are to *Life in Britain Between the Wars*):

Richard Aldington, *Soft Answers*, copyright © by Madame Catherine Guillaume, Rosica Colin Ltd., p. 22.

Sir John Betjeman, 'Middlesex' from *Collected Poems*, John Murray Ltd., p. 144.

The Editor, *Decorative Art, The Studio Yearbook, 1933*, Studio Vista Ltd., p. 154.

Louis MacNiece, 'Interregnum', *New Statesman*, p. 198.

Charles Masterman, *England after the War*, Hodder & Stoughton Ltd., pp. 19, 23–24.

J. B. Priestley, *English Journey*, William Heinemann Ltd., p. 166.

Beatrice Webb, *Beatrice Webb's Diaries*, The London School of Economics and Political Science, p. 40.

Lord Winterton, *Orders of the Day*, Cassell & Co. Ltd., Raymond Savage Ltd., p. 37.

Dornford Yates, *Berry & Co.*, The Executors of the Estate of the late Dornford Yates, pp. 18–19.

The author and publisher would also like to thank the following for permission to reproduce the illustrations in this book:

Aerated Bread Co. Ltd. for fig. 22; Architectural Review for fig. 104; Associated Press Ltd. for figs. 125, 129; British Broadcasting Corporation for figs. 46, 49; British Music Hall Society for fig. 53; Montague Burton Ltd. for fig. 19; Butlins Ltd. for fig. 110; W. A. Camwell for fig. 91; Central Press Photos Ltd. for figs. 108, 123, 124, 130; Colgate-Palmolive Publicity for fig. 82; Condé Nast Publications Ltd. for fig. 75; Daily Express for figs. 79, 115; Daily Mail for figs. 9, 80; Daily Mirror for fig. 121; Evening News for fig. 78; Fox

The Illustrations

I

After the Deluge

People and politicians alike were taken by surprise when the First World War ended in November 1918. As late as the middle of the summer, the Germans' 'Big Push' had nearly succeeded in breaking through the Allied defensive system in France; and even when the German advance first slackened and then turned into a retreat, it was thought that the war might not end until 1920. But, with German civilian morale at a low ebb and his army's morale shaken by the failure of their all-out effort at victory, the German commander, Ludendorff, insisted that his Government seek an armistice. At 11 a.m. on 11 November 1918 ('Armistice Day') the fighting ceased. The war was won.

Perhaps, on that day of hysterical cheering, dancing and singing in the streets, men and women felt that the sacrifices of

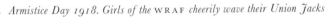

Armistice Day 1918. Girls of the WRAF *cheerily wave their Union Jacks*

A Kiddies' Tea Party celebrates the Peace Treaty, 1919, in a London street. Significantly, the mums find it difficult to look appropriately jubilant

the previous four years, including the loss by the United Kingdom of 750,000 lives, had not been in vain. If they really did think so, it was probably for the last time. True, Woodrow Wilson, President of the United States, was promising that victory would lead to a world 'made safe for democracy', and Lloyd George, the British Prime Minister, was holding out prospects of a land 'fit for heroes to live in'. But, as the cheering died away, events seemed to belie such hopes.

The first harvest of peace for many households was an exceptionally heavy bout of influenza. The epidemic, called for no sound reason the 'Spanish flu', ravaged the land in the winter of 1918–19 and caused 150,000 deaths. The second phenomenon of a world at peace was an immediate rise in prices, which went on unchecked until the end of 1920 and with which wages failed to keep pace. But when, during 1921 and 1922, prices came tumbling down again, the effects were even worse. A brief postwar boom had turned into a slump from which there was, in certain respects, no complete recovery during all the years of peace. In each of the years 1919, 1920 and 1921, more workers were involved in industrial disputes than in any other year on record except for 1926, the year of the General Strike. Nor were feelings of disillusion and resentment confined to industrial workers. Many others who had served in the ranks

16

appeared to have lost their faith in the governing class because of their conviction that lives had been uselessly sacrificed on the Western Front by the bungling incompetence of the Generals. This view was held by many of the younger ex-officers also, since the casualty rate among the junior officers, who had had to lead their men 'over the top', was so high that it was alleged that the average expectation of life of a subaltern on arrival in the trenches was little more than three weeks.

And now neither ex-soldiers nor ex-officers qualified as 'heroes'. The ex-soldier was likely to be unemployed or on strike; if unemployed he was considered lazy or unemployable, and if on strike he was either an 'agitator' or a victim of Bolshevik propaganda. The young ex-officer was made aware that service in the trenches, perhaps the only occupation he had had since leaving his public school at 18, was no passport to civilian employment. At best, a youth made old by experience of trench warfare found it hard to re-establish relations with older people, who still regarded him as the schoolboy he had been when he first left for the front; or who lectured him on the need to forget the 'good times' and the 'adventure' he had had in the army and to settle down to a steady job. But the prospects of remunerative employment shrank for ex-officers, too, when the boom collapsed in 1921. Too many saw their gratuities dribble away in rather pathetic ventures into agricultural small-holding or chicken-farming. The division between those who had served at the front and those who had stayed at home was all the greater because the stay-at-homes had had hardly any of that experience of being under direct enemy fire that air attack gave to civilians between 1939 and 1945. They had almost no

Ex-service men playing barrel organs displaying pictures of wife and children, statements of war service and appeals for work were a commonplace in the London streets of the twenties

comprehension of the realities of the war; and the men who came back almost all preserved a great silence on the subject. Only with the flood of war books that came at the end of the 1920s did civilians at last begin to understand something of what men in uniform had really endured.

Some of this discontent found expression in a widespread belief in the existence of an allegedly large group of war profiteers, often of alien origin. This idea, together with many other upper-class phobias of the early twenties, is amusingly illustrated in the writings of the popular author of the period, Dornford Yates. Himself an ex-officer, he created in his books a family group of charming people living in an historic country house in Hampshire, called 'White Ladies'. The family have many madcap misadventures, almost all brought about by the stupidity or greed of foreigners, crooks, domestic servants and the lower classes in general. Their reaction on learning, in the course of a volume called *Berry and Co.* (published in 1936 and reprinted ten times by 1950), that their neighbour's estate is up for auction, reveals much of the state of mind of the year 1919 in which the story is set:

A terrible fellow's after it. One Dunkelsbaum. Origin doubtful—very. Last known address, Argentina. Naturalized in July, 1914. Strictly neutral during the war, but managed to net over a million out of cotton, which he sold to the Central Powers *at a lower price than Great Britain offered* before we tightened the blockade. Never interned, of course. . . .

Merry Down was the nearest estate to White Ladies, and was almost as precious to us as our own home. For over two centuries a Bagot had reigned uninterruptedly over the rose-red mansion and the spreading park, the brown water and the waving woods—a kingdom of which we had been free since childhood. . . .

One of the old school, Sir Anthony had stood his ground up to the last. The War had cost him dear. His only son was killed in the first months. His only grandson fell in the battles of the Somme. His substance, never fat, had shrunk to a mere shadow of its former self. The stout old heart fought the unequal fight month after month. Stables were emptied, rooms were shut up, thing after thing was sold. It remained for a defaulting solicitor to administer the *coup de grâce*. . . . On the twelfth day of August . . . Merry Down was to be sold by auction. . . .

'D'you mean to say that this is what I fought for?' said I. 'For this brute's peaceful possession of Merry Down?'

'Apparently,' said my brother-in-law. 'More. It's what Derry Bagot and his boy died for, if you happen to be looking at it that way.'

But, since this is fiction, Berry and Co. encompass the defeat of the dreadful Dunkelsbaum. They meet him in the way, drive him several miles in the wrong direction, deposit him in a deep ford and, after more schoolboy fun at his expense, prevent his ever reaching the sale. The outcome was as satisfactory a piece of wish-fulfilment as could be desired:

> . . . the purchaser, who had paid a good price, was of English blood, and had known Derry Bagot at Eton, and soldiered with him first in South Africa and afterwards in France. The place had passed into good, clean hands and was to be well cared for.

There was substance in this picture of a landed aristocracy in decline; and it was much in the minds of more serious contemporaries. Charles Masterman, the Liberal MP whose *Condition of England* had attempted a comprehensive social survey of the England of 1908, wrote a similar survey called *England after the War* in 1922. In it he provides a reminder that 'Derry Bagot' was not unique: 'In the retreat from Mons and the first battle of Ypres perished the flower of the British aristocracy. . . . In the useless slaughter of the Guards on the Somme or of the Rifle Brigade in Hooge Wood, half the great families of England, heirs of large estates and wealth, perished without a cry.' Nor was the sale of Merry Down unique. Masterman wrote: 'in one year, one firm of auctioneers declare they have disposed of the area of an English county. I note that sales are being announced every day in the newspapers, of historic country houses and of estates running into many thousands of acres.'

Colour was also given to the belief that wealth in England was passing into the hands of 'hardfaced men' who had 'done well out of the war', often as contractors to the Government, by the exceptional number of businessmen who held office in Lloyd George's Ministry at the time and by the number of other business figures to whom he gave titles. It was felt that Lloyd George bestowed these titles on persons of dubious character and that during his premiership, particularly between 1918 and 1922, titles could be obtained from the Government in return for cash payments. The belief was sufficiently credible for an astute gentleman called Maundy Gregory to be able to make money by extracting cash from wealthy aspirants on the pretext that he could secretly transmit it to the Government, who would then confer a knighthood, baronetcy or peerage according to the amount of money handed over. But the most spectacularly shady character of the time was Horatio Bottomley, MP, a fat, several-times-bankrupt journalist-demagogue who breakfasted on kippers and champagne. He founded the weekly paper, *John Bull*, as a journal posing as the soldier's friend, airing his grievances and calling his attention unceasingly to the wickedness of those in high places. He had made rousing recruiting speeches during the war, for which he charged a large fee.

Horatio Bottomley arrives top-hatted at Bow Street to face the fraud charges that ended his career as a public benefactor

The fee was even larger when he made use of a moving peroration containing deeply-felt references to Jesus, the Prince of Peace. His total earnings for these patriotic orations was £27,000. In *John Bull* he regularly referred to the Germans as 'the Germ-Huns' and in one issue published a copy of the birth certificate of the Labour politician, Ramsay

MacDonald, in order to reveal that MacDonald was illegitimate. This was in order to discredit MacDonald's near-pacifist attitude towards the war.

Bottomley's unmasking was one of the major sensations of 1922. After great difficulty it was proved that he had converted to his own use large sums of money which he had persuaded readers of *John Bull* and others to part with, on the understanding that he would invest their offerings in the newly issued Government stock known as 'Victory Bonds'. A Victory Bond cost £5, which was more than Bottomley's victims could afford; but if they sent him 'just a quid or two' he would buy a part-share in a Bond for them. At his trial at the Old Bailey he presented himself as the innocent victim of a cruel persecution and burst into tears. He was sentenced to seven years' penal servitude. It is an odd comment, both on the man and the times, that the downfall of this uncommon swindler, who had robbed simple domestic servants, widows and the unemployed, seemed to arouse widespread sympathy.

No less disturbing to the solid mass of the public was the fact that all those young people who could afford it, and many among their elders whose incomes were not derived from land or the threatened profits of the basic industries, appeared to be indulging in 'orgies' of self-indulgent pleasure. This idea was also fostered by the Press; the word 'orgies' was used to sell both sensational newspapers and films in the twenties, and when 'orgies' ceased to titillate, recourse was had to the expression 'nameless orgies'. The small kernel of truth in this was that 1921 and 1922 saw the emergence of two notable changes in the drinking habits of the affluent, the opening of the first night-clubs in London and the début of the cocktail. The night-club shocked an older generation convinced that 'early to bed, early to rise, makes a man healthy, wealthy and wise' and the cock-tail affronted all persons with a palate for sherry or madeira by its gross misalliance of proletarian gin and dubious Latin vermouth; and anything Latin or Mediterranean was instantly suspected of degeneracy. Most degenerate of all was the jazz band. Jazz contained three elements alien to all that was 'truly British': the American, the Jewish and the Negro or, to use the crude xenophobic idiom of the time (for the twenties were harsh as well as hectic), it was all the doing of Yanks, Yids and niggers. A representatively bitter expression of the distaste aroused by the 'swinging' London of the early 1920s came from the pen of Richard Aldington, angrily contrasting the lot of the million wartime dead with that of those who survived to make merry, in a work called *Soft Answers*:

> To the sound of ten thousand jazz bands, with the ominous tom-tom undertone beating on the nerves, those sinister years shuffled and shimmied their dance of death. When evening twilight sank with heart-shaking sadness over the million silent graves, already the taxis and cars crowded the streets, hurrying to restaurants and parties; all night the restless feet slid and stamped, and the niggers grinned over the drums, and the joyless rejoiced without joy; and at dawn, when the wind breathed an immense sigh over the cross-marred desolate fields, the feet still stamped and voices still shouted for more drink, and paler cheeks more plainly showed the smear of reddened lips. A happy time. You could almost hear the rattle of the bones in this macabre pageant, dulling thought and feeling like a villainous drug, which had always to be renewed in larger and longer doses.

A similar distaste lay not far below the polished surface of the lyrics and plays of Noel Coward, was a principal theme in Aldous Huxley's early novels and given more temperate but perhaps more permanent expression in the works of T. S. Eliot, whose *The Waste Land* was published in that same critical year of 1922.

Yet this atmosphere of non-stop cocktail shaking and all-night dancing to jazz bands was largely confined to the West End of London. It was possible, even at the time, by too close a study of the popular Press or too eager an absorption in the works of 'advanced' writers, to conclude that Christianity was almost extinct, that marriage was an outmoded convention, that the dawn of complete sexual freedom had already broken and that the Victorian virtues of public-spiritedness, thrift and

The Dancing Twenties. Two lady diners wear the fashionable 'cloche' hats of 1926; others leave their fur coats hung over the chair

hard work had all been relegated to the past. The truth was different. The majority of the English at that time saw the characteristic iconoclasms of the twenties with alarm. They retained a deep attachment to all those qualities of the prewar past that clever people were most assiduously deriding. And not only was there regret that the world was changing, there was anger. There was the anger of Berry and Co. at the loss of wealth and status by those whose links were with the land; there was the anger of the employing class against the wage-earners' intransigent resistance to attempts to keep down their standards of living and against their increasing tendency to vote Labour; the anger of the industrialist who was not doing well against financiers who were not doing at all badly. And, perhaps above all, there was the anger of the middle class, of the vast numbers living in suburbia and outer suburbia who felt themselves to be 'the new poor'. Masterman depicted a typical suburb, calling it 'Richford', and wrote of it:

> Richford hates and despises the working classes, as all Rich-fords hate and despise the working classes . . . partly because it has contempt of them, and partly because it has fear of them. . . . It is chiefly opposed to Government when that Government is 'truckling' to Labour. Labour represents for

it literally the figure of the Bolshevik of the cartoons, an un-washed, ill-dressed, truculent immigrant from the neighbour-ing Labour cities; tearing up the tree-avenues of its streets, trampling on its flower-beds, thrusting its clumsy feet through the bow-windows and aspidistra of its front drawing-rooms. In the face of such a vision, it falls back on the protection of Government. . . . For Government, at worst, protects the hutch, the kennel and the safe breeding-ground; and life is a hazardous and difficult business outside.

Of the 'new poor' he wrote: 'It is this Middle Class . . . which everywhere from the clergyman or Civil Servant or medical man at the top to the small shopkeeper or the clerk at the other end of the scale is being harassed out of existence by the finan-cial after-consequences of war. . . . They had been far more hardly hit than the working man by the immense increase of prices.' The bottom had fallen out of their world, he insisted, because that world had been founded on the belief that 'a sudden doubling of prices was as unlikely to occur during its lifetime as the opening of a volcano in the middle of its streets'.

It is not surprising, therefore, that by 1922 these multitudi-nous alarms produced a crisis in the political world. In an election held in 1918 immediately after the Armistice, Lloyd George, as 'The Man Who Won The War', had been returned as Prime Minister at the head of a Coalition Government with a large majority. Unfortunately, Lloyd George had little real Party backing in the Commons. Nominally a Liberal, he had alienated the Liberals by unseating Asquith as Prime Minister in 1916; and though a great Radical, he had quarrelled with the Labour Party which, though still small and ineffective, had become the largest Party of Opposition in 1918. His position as Prime Minister depended on the Conservative majority in the Commons; and by 1922, though almost all the Conservative leaders still supported him, the Party as a whole wanted to be rid of him. He was the most constructive British statesman of the century, and the postwar Coalition had many achievements to its credit; but Lloyd George's methods were considered devious, disorganized, unpredictable and unprincipled. The continuing respect for him which was expressed by such impressive witnesses as Churchill, Balfour and Austen Chamberlain suggests that some of the calumnies propagated about him then and since originated in the kind of party-political spite of which Asquith was a somewhat more dignified victim. Lloyd George had, however, pursued policies in

'The Man Who Won the War.' Lloyd George, driven from office in 1922 and kept out of it for the rest of his life

Europe, Ireland, Egypt, Turkey and India which greatly upset the Conservatives without pleasing their opponents; and he had failed to solve the problems of industrial unrest and uncertainty at home. At a momentous Party meeting at the Carlton Club in October 1922, the Conservatives voted to withdraw support from him. Lloyd George at once resigned, and never again held political office, though he did not die until 1945. In the general election that followed, the Conservatives, led by Bonar Law, were returned to power with a handsome majority, for the first time since 1905. Significantly, Bonar Law's election slogan had been the word 'Tranquillity'.

Although Bonar Law had been the official leader of the Conservative revolt against Lloyd George, the man whose voice had been most effective at the Carlton Club was Stanley Baldwin; and when Bonar Law died in 1923, Baldwin succeeded him as Prime Minister. In 1922 Baldwin, although an MP since 1908, and already 55, was no more than a little-known junior Minister in Lloyd George's Government. When it was learned that he intended unseating Lloyd George if he could, he was likened to 'the cabin-boy' rebelling against the ship's captain; when he was made Prime Minister it was widely believed that he had been accurately described as a man 'of the utmost insignificance'. Yet this unspectacular, ruminative man so imposed his personality upon the whole period after 1922 that it

25

has, with pardonable exaggeration, been called 'The Baldwin Age'.

Baldwin's most important characteristic was that, like the other two Prime Ministers of the time, Ramsay MacDonald and Neville Chamberlain, men with whom he worked with perfect amity, his mind had been moulded by an upbringing that was not modern, intellectual or metropolitan, but Late Victorian, stolidly middle class and almost wholly provincial. Baldwin himself was a provincial, middling businessman; Ramsay MacDonald was an illegitimate Scot with a hankering after the way of life of a minor Edwardian country gentleman; Neville Chamberlain was a provincial businessman of Unitarian beliefs and a hatred of all forms of ostentation. Born in the 1860s, all three of them carried forward into the 1920s and 1930s the attitudes of a more stable and less strident past. This made them, for good as well as for ill, representative of the great mass of Englishmen; for that mass too was unaffected by the advanced thinkers, the 'smart' the 'fast' and the 'sophisticated' and equally suspicious—on balance, far too suspicious—of innovators, whether in politics and economics, or in literature, art and manners.

Baldwin and Mrs Baldwin, 1924. 'Mr Churchill,' said a society hostess, 'have you seen Mrs Baldwin's hats?' Baldwin's own lack of smartness drew pained comment from The Tailor and Cutter

That Baldwin's influence in particular spread far beyond the narrow confines of the political world and affected the attitudes of many quite ordinary people was due to the fact that he and Mac-Donald were the first men to be at the head of affairs in the new era of mass communications. They were the first Prime Ministers to be reported and pictured in newspapers that sold by the million, who were seen on cinema newsreels by anything up to 20 million people a week and could be heard from time to time on wireless sets that were also numbered by the million. The mass media that made Hitler and Mussolini so inescapable in their countries served also to imprint upon the English mind of the time the safe, solid face of Stanley Baldwin and the reassuringly sentimental features of the good-looking Ramsay MacDonald.

Baldwin had no administrative gifts. If Lloyd George, as Churchill said, was unequalled at getting things done, Baldwin was often unequalled at doing nothing. His aims were simple, and frequently formulated in speeches of much felicity. First, he wanted to get back to what he called 'clean' government. Second, he determined to restrain the petulant and provocative anti-Socialism of his Tory back-benchers. Third, he wanted to woo the Labour Party into acceptance of Parliamentary methods as the only way in which to achieve their aims. He was, therefore, frequently criticized by his own Party, greatly respected by his opponents and, until 1935, immensely popular in the country. His view of the past as a kind of idyllic industrial counterpart to the White Ladies of Berry and Co. is illustrated by the occasion in 1925 when he took the heat out of a bad-tempered Parliamentary debate about trade unions by describing the old kind of family business where 'nobody ever got the sack' and where 'a number of old gentlemen used to spend their days sitting on the handles of wheelbarrows smoking their pipes'. He once said in a broadcast, 'I sometimes think if I were not leader of the Conservative Party I should like to be the leader of the people who do not belong to any party.' In 1925 *The Times* wrote of Baldwin, 'It is the fragrance of the fields, the flavour of apple and hazel nut, all the unpretentious, simple, wholesome, homely but essential qualities, suggestions and traditions of England that Mr Baldwin has substituted for the over-charged, heavy-laden decadent atmosphere of post-war days.'

It might have been Berry and Co. celebrating the defeat of Dunkelsbaum: 'The place had passed into good, clean hands and was to be well cared for.'

MacDonald Triumphant. A Rally to celebrate the First Labour Government of 1924. On his left, Margaret Bondfield, later the first woman cabinet minister, and J. H. (Jimmy) Thomas, creator of the N. U. R.

All the same, Baldwin had no easy passage through the minefields of twenties' politics. Six months after becoming Prime Minister in 1923, he dissolved Parliament, held an election on the issue of Protection, and lost. He claimed that the protection of British industry against foreign competition by the imposition of tariffs, or import duties, was the only way to prevent unemployment. The Liberals and the Labour Party were at once able to claim that the Tories wanted to put up prices and tax the people's food. As a result, in the new Parliament the Tories, with 258 seats, were outnumbered by Labour, with 191, and the Liberals with 159. Baldwin could not, therefore, continue in power, but since neither he nor Asquith (who led all the Liberals by now) had any relish for Coalitions, it was agreed that Labour should form a Government and that the Liberals would give it general support; though subject to its good (i.e. non-Socialist) behaviour. The first Labour Government held office from January to October 1924.

This event, like the ascendancy of Baldwin, also helped to take some of the angry apprehension out of English life and politics. Some hoped, and others feared, that the advent of a Labour Government heralded revolution. The reality was different. What happened in 1924 was that Labour was absorbed into the existing social and political order by being given official status as the natural alternating Party to the Conservatives. Henceforward, Labour politicians for the most part ceased even to pretend to be rebels; they became potential Cabinet Ministers (or ex-Cabinet Ministers) instead. To none was this transformation more welcome than to Labour's Prime Minister, Ramsay

MacDonald. Of considerable Parliamentary experience, he thought of himself primarily as a statesman, and for choice an international statesman, which was why he was his own Foreign Secretary. The most 'Socialist' thing about him was his belief in the League of Nations, disarmament and international co-operation, causes which he served well for as long as harsh circumstances permitted. From the point of view of the electorate his outstanding assets were his physical appearance, which was accounted handsome, and his heart-warming Scottish accent. This, while clearly demonstrating that he did not belong to the English governing class, did not arouse the hostility, derision or condescending amusement with which the English are accustomed to regard other regional or national accents. The content of his speeches was as acceptable as his manner; he was usually more cosily vague even than Baldwin.

The first Labour Government was a landmark nevertheless, or at least a portent; and since he was a straightforward, fair-minded man of great common sense, King George V's comments spoke for many outside Buckingham Palace. After conversations with the only left-winger in the Government, the Glasgow printer, John Wheatley, the King commented, 'I should have felt exactly as he does if I had had his sort of childhood.' In general, the Labour Ministers of 1924 revealed for the first time that the traditional English view that an intelligent amateur could perfectly well preside over a great Government department also applied even when the amateurs were not 'gentlemen' but former textile operatives, foundry-workers, coal-miners or engine-drivers. Here again, George V expressed the puzzled surprise this caused; he wrote to his mother, Queen Alexandra, 'I must say they all seem to be very intelligent and they take things very seriously. They have different ideas to ours as they are all socialists, but they ought to be given a chance & ought to be treated fairly.'

But, of course, enough was enough; and when MacDonald proposed to adopt the sensible policy of developing not only diplomatic but also commercial relations with the Soviet Union, Parliamentary opposition mounted and he decided to go to the country. Always much less ready to be 'soft' with Labour than

CIVIL WAR PLOT BY SOCIALISTS' MASTERS.

MOSCOW ORDERS TO OUR REDS.

GREAT PLOT DISCLOSED YESTERDAY.

"PARALYSE THE ARMY AND NAVY."

AND MR. MACDONALD WOULD LEND RUSSIA OUR MONEY!

DOCUMENT ISSUED BY FOREIGN OFFICE

AFTER "DAILY MAIL" HAD SPREAD THE NEWS.

A "very secret" letter of instruction from Moscow, which we publish below, discloses a great Bolshevik plot to paralyse the British Army and Navy and to plunge the country into civil war.

The letter is addressed by the Bolsheviks of Moscow to the Soviet Government's servants in Great Britain, the Communist Party, who in turn are the masters of Mr. Ramsay MacDonald's Government, which has signed a treaty with Moscow whereby the Soviet is to be guaranteed a "loan" of millions of British money.

The letter is signed by Zinoviev, the Dictator of Petrograd, President of the Third (Moscow) International, and is addressed to A. MacManus, the British representative on the executive of this International, who returned from Moscow to London on October 18 to take part in the general election campaign.

Our information is that official copies of the letter, which is dated September 15, were delivered to the Foreign Secretary,

paign of disclosure of the foreign policy of MacDonald.

ARMED INSURRECTION.

The IKKI [Executive Committee, third (Communist) International] will willingly place at your disposal the wide material in its possession regarding the activities of British imperialism in the Middle and Far East. In the meanwhile, however, strain every nerve in the struggle for the ratification of the Treaty, in favour of a continuation of negotiations regarding the regulation of relations between the S.S.S.R. and England. A settlement of relations between the two countries will assist in the revolutionising of the international and British proletariat not less than a successful rising in any of the working districts of England, as the establishment of close contact between the British and Russian proletariat, the exchange of delegations and workers, etc., will make it possible for us to extend and develop the propaganda of ideas of Leninism in England and the Colonies. Armed warfare must be preceded by a struggle against the inclinations to compromise which are embedded among the majority of British workmen, against the ideas of evolution and peaceful extermination of capitalism. Only then will it be possible to count upon complete success of an armed

Zinoviev, whose real name is Apfelbaum.

insurrection. In Ireland and the Colonies the case is different; there there is a national question, and this represents too great a factor for success for us to waste time on a

letariat and desire in the future direct not the blind mechanical forces in the service of the bourgeoisie but a national army.

Form a directing operative b of the Military Section.

Do not put this off to a full moment, which may be pregnant with events and catch you unprepared.

Desiring you all success, both in organisation and in your struggle.

With Communist Greetings, President of the Presidium of the IKKI, ZINOVIEV. Member of the Presidium, McManus, Secretary, KUUSINEN.

FOREIGN OFFICE PROTEST.

REPLY WITHOUT DELAY REQUESTED.

The following is the text of the l sent yesterday by Mr. J. D. Gregory M. Rakovski, the Chargé d'Affaires London of the Soviet Union:—

FOREIGN OFFICE, October 24, 19

Sir,—I have the honour to invite attention to the enclosed copy of a l which has been received by the Central Committee of the British Communist Party from the Presidium of the Executive Committee of the Communist International, over the signature of Monsieur Zinoviev, its president, dated September 15.

The letter contains instruction British subjects to work for the violent overthrow of existing institutions this country, and for the subversion of his Majesty's armed forces as a means to that end.

2. It is my duty to inform you his Majesty's Government cannot regard this propaganda and must regard it as a direct interference from outside in British domestic affairs.

3. No one who understands the constitution and the relationships of the Communist International will doubt intimate connection and contact the Soviet Government. No Government will ever tolerate an arrangement a foreign Government by which latter is in formal diplomatic relations of a correct kind with it, while at same time a propagandist body once ally connected with that foreign Government encourages and even orders its jects of the former to plot and plan lutions for its overthrow.

Such conduct is not only a grave parture from the rules of internati comity, but a violation of specific solemn undertakings repeatedly give his Majesty's Government.

4. So recently as June 4 of last the Soviet Government made the f ing solemn agreement with his Maje Government:—

The Soviet Government undert not to support with funds or in other form persons or bodies or age

The Daily Mail *unmasks the Red Letter and gives an identikit drawing of its alleged author. The claim that Zinoviev's 'real' name was 'Apfelbaum' was designed to assert that as well as being a Bolshevik he was also a German Jew*

Baldwin, the Press worked up a great 'scare' during the election campaign. The *Daily Mail* printed a copy of the so-called 'Zinoviev letter'. Said to have emanated from Moscow, this incited British Communists to acts of sedition in industry and among the armed forces. Although the letter referred to the Labour Party in terms of the utmost contempt, the *Daily Mail* indicated that MacDonald's plan to establish relations with Russia would flood the country with Bolshevik agitators; the electorate was urged to vote for the Conservatives and the Union Jack and not for MacDonald and the Red Flag. Thereafter, it was an article of faith among Labour supporters that the capitalist Press would always run a scare at election times. The bitterness did not go out of politics as fast as Baldwin and MacDonald hoped. Nevertheless, the permanent legacy of Labour's nine months of power worked in that direction. Henceforth, the discontented now had more than a political party of their own; they had an alternative government and, in MacDonald, an ex-Premier. Even if at times they thought the Labour Party a poor thing, at least it was their own. One day, when it got a real majority in Parliament, things would soon change for the better. And so, with the workers appeased by this thought, Baldwin, having won the election, returned as Prime Minister for another five years.

Further Reading

The most complete general account is C. L. Mowat, *Britain Between the Wars*, 1955; a more recent, shorter survey is in L. C. B. Seaman, *Post-Victorian Britain*, 1966, pages 105–303. Arthur Marwick, *The Deluge*, 1965, analyses the effects of the First World War on English society; C. F. Masterman, *England After the War*, 1922, is a somewhat overwritten but revealing contemporary assessment. Beaverbrook, *The Decline and Fall of Lloyd George*, 1963, describes the collapse of the Coalition entertainingly; G. M. Young, *Stanley Baldwin*, 1952, is readable, though regarded as inadequate. There is no satisfactory life of MacDonald.

II

Employment and Unemployment

The years between the wars were years during which the British were faced with the fact that the industries and techniques which had made them uniquely prosperous in the nineteenth century were no longer appropriate to the more competitive world of the twentieth. The inventive skill and adaptiveness of British industry and technology had been in decline before 1914. They proved exceptionally laggardly in adjusting to the radically altered world of the 1920s and 1930s.

In innocent expectation of an immediate return to prewar normality, manufacturers and financiers made plans in 1919 for a long-term boom in the demand for British goods. By the end of 1920 the boom had exhausted itself. The productive capacity of those industries on which British prosperity had been based for a hundred years was suddenly found to be wholly in excess of world demand. A Europe in postwar chaos could not afford to buy; countries outside Europe, particularly India, South Africa and Canada, having been cut off from UK products during the war, had pushed ahead with their own industrialization or sought rival sources of supply. This shrinkage of demand for British exports, and the general dislocation of world trade, drastically reduced the demand for shipping. From 1921 onwards, British shipyards contributed 40 per cent of the world's annual demand for new ships while possessing the capacity to supply more than the whole of that demand. By the mid twenties, the industry abandoned hope of ever again finding employment for more than three out of every four of its workers. The decline in the demand for shipping affected the iron and steel and engineering industries; and it reduced the demand

for coal, already lessened by the use of oil and electricity. The British coal industry was by far the largest industry in the country, employing over a million workers. Yet it was antiquated, under-mechanized and ill-organized; and many of its best seams were exhausted. Its productivity was, therefore, low and its prices uncompetitively high. To complete the

Government propaganda poster, 1920. Statistics to show that miners' wages are much bigger than owners' profits

picture of gloom, the huge traditional market for Lancashire cotton goods in India had been in great measure lost to the cotton-mills of India itself and those of the Japanese, to whom much of the China market had also been lost. In 1913 UK consumption of raw cotton was 2,178 million lb. In 1920 it was 1,726 million. In 1921 it dropped to 1,066. It never again reached the 1920 figure.

The three basic industries, coal, shipbuilding and textiles, never recovered from the slump that afflicted them by the end of 1920; and this was what gave to the interwar period the phenomenon of long-term large-scale unemployment for which it is so unhappily remembered. Unemployment due to seasonal factors, to temporary depressions or interruptions in supplies of raw materials had occurred in the past; unemployment due to the more or less continuous contraction of what had hitherto been the largest fields of industrial employment had no precedent. The shock was all the greater for its dramatic appearance after the wartime years when there had been full employment and when wage increases had more than kept pace with the rise in prices. The army's insistence on paying part of a soldier's pay direct to his wife meant that in some households a higher proportion of the man's income was available (and more regularly available) than before. Moreover, many skilled workers had escaped the war altogether in order to man the essential industries and they had enjoyed a marked increase in prosperity. When, therefore, so soon after the war, there was sudden unemployment and a general drive to reduce wages, feelings were understandably bitter. In 1920 Unemployment Insurance was extended to all workers earning less than £5 a week (unless they were agricultural workers or domestics); and in 1921 provision was made for men to go on drawing benefit after their entitlement under the insurance scheme was exhausted. This 'uncovenanted' benefit, as it was officially called, was nicknamed 'the dole', though 'being on the dole' soon came simply to mean being unemployed. Without these provisions, it is hard to see how revolution could have been avoided. The unemployed were 'kept alive', wrote a contemporary, 'by "doles" from the Government, issued by the Labour Exchanges. Others have money or groceries flung at them by the Boards of Guardians, who profess . . . that amongst the thousands of applicants they are utterly unable to discriminate between the deserving and the undeserving.'

Among some families even these palliatives barely averted starvation. It was reported from a poor part of Birmingham that a 'very large item' in the diet of elementary schoolchildren was 'raw carrots and raw swedes'. A health visitor's case-book contained the following from the same area:

Mrs J.'s husband's been out of work 14 weeks and there's five of them starving on 15s. a week. . . . Mrs J., a young woman of 26 had, as the neighbours said, 'gone away almost to a skeleton' through sheer starvation. Though she was nursing

Unemployed queue for the dole, 1924

Wigan during the 1921 coal strike

her baby, I found that all the food she herself had had yesterday was a cup of tea at breakfast-time, and tea and two slices of bread and butter, provided by a married sister living near, at tea-time. . . . From the husband's unemployment pay of £1, 5s. a week had to go to pay off a debt, 6s. 3d. for rent, and only 8s. 9d. was left for food and fire. A school dinner for the eldest child was divided with his four-year-old brother every day and saved them from utter starvation.

By June 1921 the number of registered unemployed had risen to over 2 million. From 1922 to 1929 the figure varied between 1·1 million and 1·75 million. It rose to 2 million once more in 1930 and to over 2·75 million in 1933. It did not fall below 2 million until 1936; and on the eve of the Second World War in 1939 still stood at over 1·25 million. Not surprisingly the earliest response to the situation was a wave of strikes which was in many ways a resumption on a larger scale of the industrial strife which had embittered the last years before the war. There were two police strikes, a national railway strike, two national coal strikes, violent demonstrations by unemployed in many of the larger cities, a three-month engineering strike and a two-month shipbuilding strike. In 1920 a London dock strike to stop the Government sending arms to Poland for use against the Bolsheviks brought a brief but serious danger of a revolutionary general strike.

Miners at work, 1927: waiting at a South Wales pithead after an explosion had killed fourteen nightshift workers

Primarily, the strikes were against wage reductions, an attempt to retain the higher living standards enjoyed during wartime. But, with falling prices and rising unemployment, the strike weapon proved unavailing. From 1922 to 1925 there was little industrial unrest, the loss of wages being softened by a fall in the cost of living and unemployment eased by the dole. But by 1925 there was another downswing in trade and a campaign began among industrialists to force wages down again. Only in this way, they alleged, could prices be lowered and exports be made competitive. When the coal-owners threatened a lock-out in 1925 if the miners refused wage reductions, a general strike in support of the miners' resistance seemed inevitable. It was averted when Baldwin provided a subsidy to maintain existing wages and profits while a Royal Commission examined the industry. This looked like surrender by Baldwin; but the Government used the breathing-space to appoint Commissioners to organize plans up and down the country for the maintenance of food and supplies if a general strike did in fact occur. And occur it did when, in 1926, the Royal Commission recommended, among other things, a cut in miners' wages. The Miners' Federation refused all negotiations; its secretary, A. J. Cook, chose as his battle-cry the slogan, 'Not a penny off the pay, not a minute on the day'. The TUC's undertaking to call a general strike to aid the miners had originally been made in the hope that it would prove enough of a deterrent to force the Government to intervene on the miners' behalf. It therefore negotiated with Baldwin's Government, though greatly hampered by the refusal of both miners and owners to negotiate on any terms, and by the Government's view that a general strike was tantamount to civil rebellion. Perhaps overborne by the hard-liners in his Cabinet, Baldwin brought on the strike by himself breaking off the negotiations on a flimsy pretext.

On 4 May 1926, three days after the miners had stopped work, the population woke to find themselves faced with what many feared was the prelude to Revolution. Railwaymen and dockers, road transport workers and printers, builders and engineers, together with many of the workers in the gas and electricity companies, all instantly answered the TUC's summons to strike. Just as enthusiastically, patriotic persons of all sorts volunteered to drive buses and trains; and within a week about 250,000 men had enrolled as special constables. The Government had no difficulty in finding lorries and vans to move supplies or the personnel to drive them. Lord Winterton, a Tory MP appointed as Commissioner to organize supplies in the well-heeled counties of Oxfordshire and Buckinghamshire, wrote subsequently, 'Men and women of all classes thronged to our . . . offices offering to drive cars, to move food and goods, or do any other work required. On the last day of the strike, I had 10,000 more voluntary workers than I could find work for. One lot of young wage-earners from a certain village asked to be sent as special constables to Glasgow . . . "to have a crack at them dirty bolshies on the Clyde".' Undergraduates deserted their rooms at Oxford and Cambridge to 'do their bit' as volunteers and their sisters ran canteens. It was perhaps the last occasion

Police (striped jerseys) play football with strikers during the General Strike—

in English history when the classes arrayed themselves against each other as out-and-out opponents. Certainly, it is unlikely, if a general strike had occurred ten years later, that the universities would have sent quite so many volunteers to the Government side and so few to the workers'. In 1926 the unquestioning faith with which organized workers followed their union leaders, recalling as it did their rush to join Kitchener's army in 1914, was matched by the equally unquestioning faith of the rest of the community that it was their duty to help the Government to keep the country going. Even those who did not feel impelled to contribute positively still showed what stuff the English were made of by walking or cycling or cadging a lift to work, all in a cheerful spirit that looked back to the days when Tommy had packed up his troubles in his old kitbag and smiled, smiled, smiled, and forward to the 'Britain Can Take It' spirit of the wartime Blitz.

Though there was no loss of life during the strike, there were many minor acts of violence, and some severe punishments were imposed by the more patriotic JPs. But the incident the

—but clear the streets with batons at Elephant and Castle, London—

popular mind treasured most was the football match between police and strikers organized by the Chief Constable of Plymouth; and perhaps this was because the incident symbolized the basic truth of it all: that a general strike that was only a general strike was an ineffective weapon and that both sides knew as much. If the strike was to force the Government to take the miners' side it would have to be prolonged until it produced social and economic breakdown and then violence. The TUC realized this so well that

—while lady helpers 'do their bit' at the canteens for volunteer workers in Hyde Park

behind-the-scenes negotiations went on all through the strike; and on the ninth day they called it off on terms that amounted to unconditional surrender. By this submission, the TUC committed itself to the abandonment of the general strike as a weapon, and made what amounted to a full and public repudiation of the idea of social revolution. Baldwin's victory forced the TUC back into the role of a vested interest within the existing social system; the Labour Party had been wooed into respectability, and now the TUC had been humiliated into it. For the rest of the period the movement was as conservative as any other British institution; so tamed was it that Low, the outstanding political cartoonist of the 1930s, regularly depicted the TUC as a lumbering, slumbering cart-horse.

The ending of the General Strike saved neither striking workers from victimization nor the miners from personal disaster. Their leaders still refused to negotiate and the Government lacked the will to act against the owners. The miners stayed out until November when, district by district, they dribbled back to work, almost invariably on terms involving lower pay and longer hours. To what extent the miners were driven back by 'starvation' it is hard to tell. As late as October, in the mining town of Seaham in County Durham, Beatrice Webb, the Fabian Society's *grande dame*, who was inclined to sympathize with miners' wives (though not with their husbands) reported:

> The surface facts show no exceptional distress: indeed the pit villages look clean and prosperous and the inhabitants healthy (death-rate unusually low). Various people told us that the men and boys had benefited by the rest, sun, and open air and abstinence from alcohol and tobacco (the MOH added 'from over-heating'). And the women freed from coal-dust and enjoying regular hours; whilst the schoolchildren, through the ample supply of first-class food (eleven meals each week at a cost of 3s. 6d. per child at wholesale prices) were certainly improved in health and happiness. The one want was clothing and boots, and our gift of £100 to the Repair Fund was much appreciated. From the early hours of the morning until late at night there was a continual rumbling of handbarrows past our hotel at Roker; and on the roads there were always long lines of push cycles going to and fro with bulging bags of slack and coal to the miners' homes, or peddling the stuff to other workers.
>
> The state of mind of the miners and their wives was less easy to discover than the state of their health. . . . They [the women] all seemed in good spirits, hard at work running relief funds and collecting money by whist drives, football matches (women players), dances and socials; they had raised, in the last two months, £1,700 for the central relief fund for pregnant and lying-in women and infants. Some of the lodges were paying a few shillings a week to the unmarried men; the Guardians were paying 12s. a week to the wives and 4s. a week (3s. 6d. deducted for school meals) to each child. . . . There was certainly no sign of strain. I looked at the gathering of 400 miners' wives and daughters, in their best dresses, and the pretty decorated tea-tables, with piles of cake and bread-and-butter, it might have been a gathering of prosperous lower middle-class women . . . their clothes were certainly quite as respectable and attractive. Neither were they gloomy —they were in a jolly talkative state of mind; they were enjoying their lives.

Mrs Webb, of course, was mentally comparing the scene before her in 1926 with conditions some 40 years earlier which had been much worse; and since she was 'a lady' miners' wives would know better than to embarrass her by pleading poverty or by showing her anything but their best manners, let alone their best clothes. Nor should one overlook her manifest unease at the circumstance that miners' wives in their best clothes should look like 'prosperous lower middle-class women'. The alarm of the well-to-do at the rising standards of life of what the Victorians had called 'the labouring poor' is a constant factor throughout twentieth-century history and at no time was it more freely expressed than in the twenties. What the miners were fighting for—and what the General Strike was about—was the maintenance of the rise in the standard of living among the workers that had begun during wartime. But even to Mrs Webb, nominally a Socialist, it was contrary to the fitness of things that miners' wives should look like the prosperous lower middle class. And it is clear, too, from her account, that the miners themselves were a good deal less brightly well behaved. She thought them 'silent and sullen' and was enraged that 'A. J. Cook was everywhere acclaimed a hero'. 'That inspired fool', she commented, 'is like the gangrenous gas of a badly wounded body.'

Neither Mrs Webb nor the even less sympathetic majority of the population saw the miners for what they really were—an embattled community that felt itself to be fighting in a just cause, and all the more determined to put a brave face on it now that they had been deserted by their fellow workers. And it was the breaking of their spirit, not the prim calculation of their receipts in strike pay and Poor Relief that was the real issue. But, though they deprived the nation of its coal for as long as half a year, they were defeated. The victory of the owners' policy of longer hours and lower wages enabled the industry to stagger on in its old inefficient, out-of-date fashion and thus postponed its reorganization and modernization for another 20 years. The events of 1926, when viewed from one aspect, represent a triumph for sanity and moderation; from the miners' side they added up to a tragedy for almost all the families of the largest single body of workers in the country.

The extent to which revolutionary or even new ideas had been smothered in the twenties was fully revealed by the nation's reactions to the onset of the World Depression from 1929 onwards. Early that year the Labour Party was considered to be so safe that, as a result of the 1929 election, it became the largest party in the Commons (though still without a majority) and MacDonald returned to Downing Street. Prices had continued to fall, and living standards outside the worst-hit regions crept up; in retrospect, the General Strike seemed an isolated irrelevancy in the otherwise calm and almost golden era of stability that had gone on since the end of 1922. So highly did the populace value this calm and stability that they hardly departed from it even when the Depression was at its worst, and showed by their votes in 1931 that they wanted absolutely nothing to be changed.

TRAMSAY.

The second Labour Government, 1929–31, had neither a majority nor a policy. Mac-Donald is shown tamely submitting to the Tories, the Liberals and the Lords. The cartoonist, Low, depicts himself (with dog) as one of MacDonald's disillusioned 'excursionists'

The Depression began in 1929 and the most spectacular event was the Wall Street Crash in New York in October of that year.

Within the next four years world trade dropped by almost a half, partly because of the cessation of the American loans that had kept it going and partly because of the overproduction of primary and other commodities in proportion to the economic demand for them. The excessive concentration of the world's gold in the United States throughout the twenties had meant that the rest of the world was too poor to buy US goods. Therefore US industrial production slumped, with the result that the demand for all the primary products of industry slumped too—cotton, rubber, tin, for example. In industrial countries, men were hungry because they had been sacked from industries choked with products nobody could pay for. In non-industrial countries and areas, men went hungry because the factories did not want their raw materials, and unemployed factory workers could not afford to buy their food products. By 1933 the League of Nations recorded a world total of 30 million unemployed. In a sense, Britain fared less badly than other countries. The US had 14 million unemployed, Germany 6 million; the UK, having been underproducing, got off with a maximum of 3 million in 1932. But since, even after 1935, by which time the country was considered to have 'recovered', the figure did not drop much below 2 million, the effect of the Depression was that unemployment became for certain individuals, and in some cases for certain whole communities, a permanent way of life throughout the thirties.

Almost everywhere else in the world the Depression produced drastic responses: Roosevelt inaugurated a New Deal for the United States, Hitler rose to power in Germany and the Japanese plunged into war in Manchuria. But all that happened in England was that instead of being governed by Baldwin and MacDonald alternately, the country elected in 1931 to be governed by both of them simultaneously. And the purpose of this decision was not to deal with the basic problems of the Depression but to cope with a financial crisis whose significance was much exaggerated.

The withdrawal of US loans to Germany and Austria after the Wall Street Crash led to financial chaos in those countries and then to a heavy drain of gold from the Bank of England.

43

To maintain foreign confidence in sterling, a loan was sought from New York. But the New York bankers announced their lack of confidence in Britain's financial position, and in its Labour Government, by refusing a loan until the British Government had balanced its Budget. It had just been made known that the Government was overspending at a rate in excess of £120 million a year. But if the loan were not forthcoming, the Bank might not be able to meet its obligations to its creditors, the pound sterling would have to go off gold and thereafter (so it was believed) fall so disastrously in value in relation to other currencies as to become almost worthless. The Budget would, therefore, have to be balanced by drastic cuts in Government expenditure. Britain's own bankers, financial experts and Treasury officials agreed wholeheartedly with the view of the US bankers.

To save the country's finances from total ruin, therefore, MacDonald and his leading colleagues planned to cut expenditure by reducing the pay of the armed forces, civil servants and school-teachers and by reducing unemployment pay by 10 per cent. MacDonald faced a dilemma: he discovered that, though the Opposition regarded his cuts as not enough, half his Cabinet refused to agree to a cut in unemployment pay. This was only to be expected: the Government had so spectacularly failed to do anything to cure unemployment that it had risen from 1 million to 2·75 million since it had been in office; and maintaining the dole was the only thing the Government could find to do for the unemployed. Unable to get his Cabinet's agreement, MacDonald brought his Government to an end; but it was announced immediately afterwards that he was to carry on as Prime Minister of a 'National' Government, containing Baldwin and Neville Chamberlain (Conservatives), Sir Herbert Samuel and Lord Reading (Liberals) and two of MacDonald's senior colleagues, Snowden and J. H. Thomas.

A fortnight later, on 10 September 1931, the cuts were duly announced by Snowden as Chancellor in an emergency Budget. Naval ratings virtually mutinied against them at Spithead and foreigners instantly took this to mean that England was about to fall into irreparable ruin. They withdrew so much more gold from the Bank that barely three weeks after being elected to preserve the gold standard, the National Government had to go off it. The pound sterling at once dropped in value by about 25 per cent—but no further. The theory—on which the whole political shake-up was based—that if the pound sterling went off gold it would become worthless—might therefore have been regarded as disproved. Nobody drew this conclusion. What they believed was that Labour, by reckless extravagance, had brought the country to the verge of ruin. Nothing but the creation of the National Government had averted that disaster; and nothing but the continuation of that Government could guarantee the country's immunity from similar perils in the future.

Sensing this feeling and anxious to capitalize on it, the Conservatives forced Baldwin and Mac-

NO MORE SOCIALIST PROMISES FOR ME, I'M VOTING NATIONAL GOVERNMENT

Election Poster, 1931. The aging workman lifts his sad old eyes up and away from his copy of Labour's newspaper, the Daily Herald. *To spare the old man's feelings, the words* 'CONSERVATIVE THIS TIME' *are seen only faintly behind* 'FOR THE NATIONAL GOVERNMENT'

Donald to go to the country, not with a policy, for the parties in the Government had opposing ideas, but with none. The electorate was asked to give the Government 'a doctor's mandate'—in other words to register a simple act of faith in the Government's capacity to restore the nation to health. People were the more moved to do this because of the behaviour of the Labour Party. As soon as MacDonald and his friends joined the National Government, the Labour Party expelled them and declared that the whole crisis was a 'bankers' ramp' and a Tory plot. When the Government had introduced its Budget, former Labour Ministers, who only a few weeks earlier had opposed only the cut in the dole,

45

announced their passionate opposition to all the cuts indiscriminately.

In the election of October 1931, the National Government secured 554 seats out of 615, and 14·5 million votes out of the 21·6 million cast. It was the largest number of seats and votes accorded to any Government in English history. Overwhelmingly, the electors voted to save themselves at the expense of soldiers, sailors, airmen, policemen, civil servants, schoolteachers and the unemployed. It is tempting to accept the later verdict of George Orwell that in 1931 the English 'all did the wrong thing in perfect unison'. MacDonald and Baldwin were hailed as men who had put country above Party. Neville Chamberlain was so moved by his Party's willingness to serve under MacDonald that he wrote, 'Truly, the Conservative Party is a wonderful embodiment of good sense, patriotism and honesty.' The remark stated, exactly, the three qualities the electors had considered themselves to be voting for. Naturally, the Labour Party took a different view. The 1931 election reduced it to a mere rump in the Commons of 52 Members; and even after the 1935 election it still had only 154 MPs. The National Government, under MacDonald till 1935, under Baldwin from then until 1937 and Neville Chamberlain thereafter, continued unassailably on, sustained till well beyond the end of the peace by the support of the majority of the electors. Only with the disasters of 1940 did more than a minority begin to suspect there might perhaps be some truth in George Orwell's description of the England of the 1930s as 'a land of snobbery and privilege, ruled largely by the old and the silly'.

Orwell's judgement was harsh. True, though its members were no older than senior politicians usually are, the National Government was almost wholly backward-looking and almost wholly representative of the prewar generation. But they were not silly, at least in their handling of domestic affairs. They were honourable, complacent men, who held the nation steady while the more or less automatic processes of recovery from a slump worked their slow effects. Though neither they nor any other politicians knew how to cure unemployment, it did not get worse; and since there were more people in work than ever before, the bulk of the population came to accept the existence of long-term unemployment in the older industrial areas in the way they accepted the phenomena of overpopulation in India or of recurrent flood and famine in China.

For, throughout the period, almost unaided and almost un-recognized by the politicians, the character of the national economy was steadily altering and producing the paradoxical fact that, despite the stagnation of basic industries, the set-backs of the General Strike and the Depression, living standards were in general rising. It was the inevitable paradox of a period of transition between two kinds of economy, and therefore between two kinds of society. Those whose skills and way of life pertained to the old economy fared badly; those whose skills served the newer forms of activity and whose way of life was served by it tended to benefit. One transition of the time was from the traditional motive power of steam to newer sources of power, the petrol engine and electricity. There was a shift from old materials to new: from basic metals to plastics (though the populace knew of these mainly in the commercial form known as 'bakelite') and from traditional natural fibres like cotton to synthetic ones such as artificial silk, with a consequent expansion of the chemical industry. Above all there began the transition from an economy dominated by heavy industry and the manufacture of capital goods to one increasingly concerned also with providing consumer goods for the masses. Thus, the production of motor cars, of artificial silk, of wood-pulp and electricity all substantially increased. A high proportion of the increased output was for the benefit of the private consumer. Other flourishing industries of the time, providing new or increased employment (and therefore purchasing power) were printing, the entertainment business and the building trades, whose output was such that a third of all the houses in the country in 1939 had been built since 1919. The building boom increased the demand for electricity, gas and water. To meet the purchasing power created by this expansion, there was an increase in the distributive trades and a great variety of new food products, from ice-cream to breakfast cereals. The number of black-coated workers rose. As the scale of commercial

47

Four guinea suits for 37/- at Burton's, Yorkshire Street, Oldham

operations and of government activity grew larger so did the number of executives, accountants, insurance clerks, civil servants and stenographers.

For the first time, therefore, the working population would be conceived of not merely as producers but also as large-scale consumers. The techniques of mass production and mass advertising at last made this possible. For the first time, there were mass-produced reading matter, entertainment, motor cars, hire-purchase furniture and radios. There were mass-produced clothes for both sexes: Montague Burton and the Fifty Shilling Tailor served the men and there were factory-made dresses for the women. Every High Street had its Woolworth's, each a poor man's (and poor woman's) treasure trove of domestic and personal gadgets and accessories, all with the comforting slogan 'Nothing Over Sixpence'. A saucepan could be bought at 6d. for the pan and 6d. for the lid, spectacles at 6d. the frame and 6d. for each lens, and the customer tested his sight free with the aid of a test card on the counter.

There were other reasons for rising living standards, among them the low prices of imports, a long-surviving legacy of the Depression. As a major importing country, Britain prospered at the expense of the foreign primary producer. The real value of wages increased in the thirties, so that any assessment of the cost of living must take account both of a national average wage of £200 a year and of very low prices. Thus, an Aerated Bread Company's teashop tariff of 1935, offering meals for shoppers and clerks in the West End of London provided two Special Lunches for 1s.: either roast beef, Yorkshire pudding and chips; or Cornish pasty, mashed potatoes, and spring greens, followed by cabinet pudding. Beans on toast cost 5½d., egg on chips 7d.;

'Nothing over Sixpence'. Woolworth's style, like Burton's, was to change little over the years; not so the prices

A 'Nippy'—a Lyons teashop waitress of the thirties. Trim, neat uniform and a face registering polite, submissive fatigue

and the extravagant customer who wanted steak and chips could have it for 1s. 3½d. Since these prices included waitress service, they demonstrate the low cost of the food, the minimal wages of the legion of waitresses, and the lack of education and opportunity which led them to be grateful for such employment.

Yet the final contribution to the increased prosperity of the many was the absolute discard of the 1·5 million wholly unemployed. The older areas of the economy did not want them; and the newer ones wanted either different skills or the nimble fingers of the new

Three-course lunch for 1/6 in an ABC teashop, London, 1932. This was probably a slightly superior establishment to the one whose 1935 prices are quoted on page 49

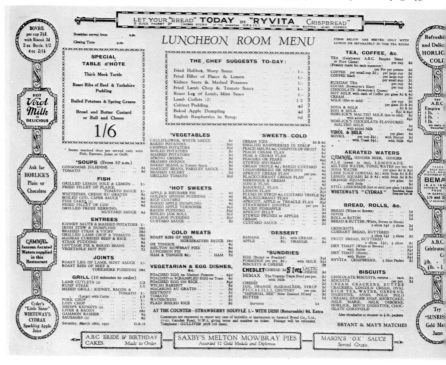

factory girl, fitting parts into electric switches and radios, or twirling decorative titbits on the tops of fancy chocolates. The unemployed got the dole; and that, in every sense, was their lot. Since their skills were not wanted and their consuming power was too low to contribute to the profits of the mass producers, even in an age of low prices, they were ignored.

Further Reading

Sidney Pollard, *Development of the British Economy 1914–67* (second edition, 1969), Chapters 3, 4 and 5. Julian Symons, *The General Strike*, 1957. Mowat, *op. cit.*, Chapters 5, 6, 7 and 8. Seaman, *op. cit.*, Chapters 10 and 16–25.

III

Modes and Morals

In matters of manners and morals, the years between the wars saw a running battle, similar to that in political and economic affairs, between those who claimed to stand for what they deemed to be the traditional values, and those who emphasized adventurousness and novelty. Although the latter were unusually vocal and active in the twenties, the traditionally minded staged a recovery in the thirties. The English in 1939 were a much staider people than an observer of the social scene in the early twenties might have expected.

One continuous factor in the changes that did take place was the changing position of women. The irrational resistance to their demand for the vote was officially abandoned in 1918, but so grudgingly that thereafter women could vote only if they were over 30, and were householders or married to householders. This discrimination was abandoned in 1928 when women were given the vote on the same terms as men, to the accompaniment of much guffawing comment in the popular Press. This reflected the characteristic middle-class, and to some extent working-class, view of women, or as they were called whenever they were mentioned at public functions, 'The Ladies, God Bless Them'. They were, when young, decorative appendages to male existence. Thereafter they were to bear and rear children. For these tasks they needed neither training nor preparation, since they were 'an instinct with them'. Unless carefully checked, they would ruin their husbands by reckless expenditure on clothes and on curtains and carpets. There was no place for them in public affairs or commerce since they had no powers of logical thought, did not understand money, were at 'certain times' in every month unfit for any activity whatever and at all other times 'too delicate'. They were also the 'modest' sex. This meant that no reference to any bodily functions should be made in their presence. No part of the human body below the neck could be named in front of them except 'arm', 'back' and 'side' (but never 'bottom', let alone 'backside') and perhaps 'figure' (which meant 'breasts') and (with diffidence) 'legs'. These ideas about women were still strongly held in the 1920s, and any departure from the modes of conduct they implied was hotly condemned.

Contrary tendencies had been at work for some time. The early safety bicycle had enabled women to escape from chaperonage, and the typewriter had got them into office work. The idea of the young working woman had been bravely defended in song before 1914 by the music-hall artiste, Miss Vesta Victoria:

> *She's no lady, some people say,*
> *Just because she goes to work*
> *For her living every day;*
> *But there's no lady*
> *More independent than she,*
> *She's just as much a lady*
> *As a lady ought to be!*

The war had for the first time diffused through most sections of society the normal working-class practice by which women and girls worked as a matter of course. During the war they had worked in factories, on the land and as bus conductresses. Their employment in factories and offices soon became normal as a result of the development of light industries, and the growth of commerce, banking and insurance, of the catering and entertainment industries and the expansion of the civil service and local government. These changes did more than provide employment for the women of the middle class; they gave working-class girls for the first time an alternative to their traditional employment as domestic servants. By 1939 Miss Vesta Victoria's point had gained universal acceptance. Married women, however, except among the lower orders, did not go

out to work. Society, though prepared to accept the new phenomenon of the financially independent spinster, was no more
ready for the financially independent wife than for the principle
of equal pay. When they married, women employed in the
public service and school-teaching, for instance, had immediately to vacate their posts. The principle that the financing of
a married household was exclusively a male responsibility was
universally maintained until 1939.

The dawning economic independence and the greater mobil-
ity of women were probably the basic reason for the revolution
in women's fashions after the war, though the growing interest
in sport also contributed. And perhaps, if women were to work
side by side with men, they ought, for safety's sake, to look less
feminine than in the past. Until 1929, brassières (they were not
yet called 'bras') were designed to flatten the bosom and not
uplift it and the prevailing shape was functionally tubular. The
truly fashionable woman appeared to possess neither breasts nor
a waist and to have neither thighs, hips nor buttocks. This effect
was made the more obvious by ludicrously low waists which,
for the most of the twenties, were fixed well below the navel.
On the other hand, women now tended to expose their arms;

*Bathing Belles at Canvey Island, Essex, 1922. The original caption read, 'A fair
bather tries to induce her chum to take to the water'*

Formal Occasion, 1922. The elderly woman is alone in not exposing her legs and in admitting to 'a figure'. The irregular hems were very fashionable. The girl on the extreme right carries a 'dorothy bag' with tassel. All the younger women have bobbed their hair.

and from 1919 to 1929 hemlines rose fairly steadily. In the former year they disclosed that above the female ankle there was the lower part of the calf; by the latter year the whole female leg was revealed as far up as the kneecap. More sensational still was the disappearance, save among that most persecuted of creatures, the schoolgirl, of black woollen stockings. Not only was wool being replaced by silk or, less expensively, by artificial silk and cotton lisle, but black was replaced by that favourite colour of the period, beige. This gave to the now freely displayed female leg the impression of publicly displayed nudity, a point tellingly confirmed by the popularity of the male joke, 'What happens to girls in black stockings? Nothing.' The allegedly 'boyish' fashions of the early 1920s looked so mostly to the older generation. To young men, the new fashions made girls look more like girls than ever, since so much more of them was publicly visible. It was thus just as well that the female contour was unalluringly flattened out, since the trunk was no longer immured in protective underclothes that could be weighed in pounds nor encased in stays, or such intimidating corsets as in

The girl, in kneelength tubular attire, strides brightly carefree; but the young man in Oxford bags is 'a bit of an ass'

the past. Silk, artificial silk or that most celebrated of between-the-wars material, crêpe de Chine, to which all aspired but relatively few could afford, reduced the weight of underwear (called by the trade 'lingerie') to ounces. By pre-war standards, and it is by those standards, and not by those of half a century later, that the fashions of the 1920s must be judged, fashionable women suddenly appeared to have become scantily dressed, pink-legged creatures with no waists, no breasts and almost no hair.

The unfashionableness of fleshly amplitude in a woman was, despite the return of curves in the thirties, perhaps made permanent by these changes of the twenties. It was connected with the new interest in games and with the sharp decline in the prewar vices of over-eating and over-drinking. Only three large ladies rose to fame in the period. Sophie Tucker, significantly known as the 'Red Hot Momma', celebrated the decline of her type by singing 'Nobody Loves a Fat Girl' ('but oh, how a fat girl can love!'). The large Irish comedienne, Tessie O'Shea, advertised herself as 'Two-Ton Tessie'; and the irrepressible Mae West, for ever remembered for her 'Come up and see me some time' and whose name was appropriately applied to the inflatable life-jackets used by airmen who 'dropped in the drink' during the Second World War, generally had to be given parts in films about the distant past because of her outrageous inappropriateness to the world around her.

Women's hair caused most controversy because, though underwear, legs and bosoms could not be mentioned freely in mixed company, hair could. The twenties saw the almost universal triumph of short hair styles. At first it was bobbed, then shingled and then, among a self-willed, daring minority, eton-cropped; and even the softer, curlier modes of the thirties still kept hair above the shoulders. It was obviously to advertise that their hair was short that women wore the close-fitting cloche hat of the twenties. In the past, a girl had celebrated the approach of womanhood by putting her hair up (arranging it in various ways like a crown instead of letting it hang girlishly down); now she proclaimed her maturity and, by implication, her emancipated disrespect for her mother, the prejudices of her father and the opinions of her headmistress and the bishops, by cutting most of it off. As a result, girls were, in the 1920s,

Seated lady, enjoying the novel amenities of a London club for women only, appreciates the deference displayed by a less emancipated member of her sex

considered as immoral and immodest for wearing their hair short as boys were for wearing it long in the 1960s. It was sometimes asserted that short hair was less troublesome to manage than long hair; but it soon turned out that short hair required frequent 'permanent waving' (first known as 'marcel waving'), and the problem got worse as curls came back. Permanent waving rapidly proved the most impermanent and most recurrent factor in a well-groomed woman's existence.

Other amazements were the increasing use of lipstick and makeup, both previously associated at best with the stage, and at worst with women of the streets. Rouge, which was more depraved still, came in more slowly. The duties which these new fashions imposed were accurately recorded by the American singer, Eddie Cantor:

> *Every morning do your stuff*
> *With a little powder and a puff. . . .*
> *If you're seen anywhere*
> *With your hat off*
> *Have a marcel wave in your hair.*

Haute Couture, 1928. Basic versions of this style were widely adopted. The hair seems to have been marcel waved

As time went on, young women created an alarmed concentration on themselves by performing the rites of the toilet in public, particularly in railway carriages at the end of long journeys. The powder-compact would be removed from the handbag. It would be snapped open, and powder from it dabbed on to the puff. The young woman would peer at her features in the compact's uplifted mirror with a stern expression, and proceed to dab at her cheeks and her nose (particularly her nose, for it must on no account be shiny) and always, it seemed, a little angrily. After that, lipstick would be applied, carefully, to achieve a cupid's-bow effect. This required the most elaborate grimacings, since the mirror was small, the train unsteady and the lips difficult to force into the exact position required for the accurate depositing of the bright red colouring matter. The outline had to be absolutely unblurred. It was unfortunate that the lipstick of the period was so indiscreet. It tended to transfer itself vividly to the rims of teacups and the cheeks of men whenever it came into contact with them.

It was naturally assumed that these new modes indicated a terrible decline in moral standards, and not until the 1960s were the guardians of tradition again to be so belligerently on the defensive. The energetic Dr Marie Stopes, who wrote books on contraceptive techniques (her most celebrated work was called *Married Love*), addressed great public meetings on the subject and opened a birth-control clinic in the Holloway Road in London; she was joked about wherever hearty males foregathered and when she brought an action against a writer who claimed she was doing it all for private profit, she lost her case and was accused in court of purveying a 'beastly, filthy message'. In 1925 the playwright, John van Druten, wrote the play *Young Woodley*, about a public schoolboy who fell romantically in love with his housemaster's young wife and aggravated the offence by reading Swinburne. The play was banned until 1928 on the grounds that it would be taken as an attack on the public schools and would cause grief and anxiety to parents. In 1928 a hardly less starry-eyed book about the sad loneliness of Lesbians, called *The Well of Loneliness*, by Miss Radclyffe Hall, was also banned, largely as the result of a campaign against it by a *Sunday Express* journalist called James Douglas. Rather than let them see this book, he declared, he would 'sooner give a healthy boy or girl a phial of prussic acid'. All three of these famous writings of the twenties were impeccably high-minded and the tone of both *Young Woodley* and *The Well of Loneliness* was ethereally romantic to the point of being, to use a word of the period, 'sloppy'.

The fashionable and intellectual worlds were extremely sex-conscious in the twenties. Freud was held to have shown that sexual activity was a necessary form of psychological hygiene; D. H. Lawrence asserted that it was supremely spiritual, but only in proportion to the extent to which it was purged of all but the physical; and, in writing so vividly about the coolly promiscuous Lucy Tantamount of his *Point Counter Point*, Aldous Huxley helped to create the false impression that she was somehow typical or at least a dread portent. At the non-intellectual level, many women (though fewer girls) swooned ridiculously over Rudolph Valentino, the slim, blank-faced young man who, in a number of silent films, either attired in riding-breeches or in the guise of a smooth ruthless 'sheikh', but in both cases likely to be carrying a whip, 'strode', as Beverley Nichols later wrote, 'through reel after reel, hurling women about as though they were sacks of potatoes and smacking them on the bottom'. The typical love scenes of the twenties were notoriously and ludicrously torrid; women would sprawl in inviting and voluptuous attitudes, the absence of sound compelling them to proclaim their amorous intent by an exaggerated rolling of their eyes and their bodies. To make the message clearer and in advance, many films were about sinuous dark-eyed Oriental beauties (*The Secrets of the Harem Revealed*). The more lurid best-sellers of the time also tended to depict women feverishly exclaiming, 'Take me and do what you will with me'.

Nevertheless, there was always far more lax sexual behaviour in books and in the imaginations of elderly moralists than in real life. For one thing, every schoolmistress in the land fought relentlessly to prevent any of her pupils developing into the cigarette-smoking, bead-jangling, fast-living female of contemporary fiction and fantasy. A schoolgirl who was overheard to use an expletive during a hockey game at any time between the wars, even *sotto voce*, would be sent instantly from the field. There are indeed grounds for considering Shaw's St Joan (the play was first performed in 1924) as a good deal more typical of the 1920s than Lucy Tantamount. Shaw's Joan was a tomboy

The Madly Romantic Look. Gladys Cooper and Ivor Novello in the play 'Iris' at the Adelphi Theatre, 1925

THAT THE TWENTIETH-CENTURY GIRL—

AFTER HAVING BOBBED HER HAIR—

THEN SHINGLED IT—

THEN ADOPTED THE ETON CROP—

NEVER QUITE REACHED THE DARTMOOR SHAVE—

AND IS NOW STARTING TO GROW IT (AND HER DRESS) AGAIN.

The demure, schoolgirly, boyish and tubular styles of the early twenties stopped before reaching the miniskirt stage and began to revert to the traditional by the end of the decade

who spoke disrespectfully to her elders and betters, dismissed their arguments with a shrug, neither cared for nor understood their preoccupation with established traditions, cut her hair short, dressed like a boy and brazenly insisted on doing a man's work in a man's world instead of the domestic chores appropriate to her sex, yet all the while treating men as asexual 'chums'. Whether Shaw's Joan belonged to the fifteenth century or not is uncertain; that she belonged to the England of the 1920s is unquestionable. Indeed, in finding something contemporary in Joan, Shaw had been anticipated by musical comedy. The Jerome Kern show, *Sally*, which reached London in 1921, had invoked Joan in one of its songs:

> *I wish I could be like Joan of Arc*
> *She was 'it' right from the start*
> *Though her pa and ma poor fishes*
> *Tried to keep her washing dishes*
> *You can't keep a good girl down!*

Even more characteristic and ingenuous were the schoolgirly girls of the time. Irrepressibly jolly, innocently coy and fancy-free, finding so much in life that was 'awfully ripping' or 'simply topping' and with so many friends who were 'absolute bricks'

61

they were short-skirted reincarnations now of Gilbert's 'Three Little Maids from School' and, at other times, of Lionel Monkton's prewar Quaker Girl, all peaches and cream, all English roses, and all longing to find, as they sang in those songs of theirs, 'a little boy who's looking for a little girl to love' so that they could settle down in 'a cottage for two', 'a room with a view' or a 'blue heaven' where 'baby makes three'.

When the nation at large received the psychological shock of the 1931 crisis and the Depression, much of the sparkle and vivacity that had given so much suspect gaiety to the twenties died away. The fashions of the 1930s were backward-looking and no longer revolutionary. A more consciously groomed appearance became the rule. The entire female sex looked as if it had suddenly grown up and got itself a well-paid job as a superior secretary or receptionist. In the twenties, girls were game for anything; in the thirties they turned back into ladies. They were sweet, neat and tidy by day and creatures of glamour in the evening. At other times they were splendidly athletic in backless swimsuit or tennis shorts, their healthy tan a consequence of the thirties' passion for sunbathing and accentuated by the vogue for sunglasses with white frames. It was of one such glowing young woman of the time that John Betjeman was thinking when he wrote 'Pam, you great big mountainous sports girl'. Curves came back in the thirties. Evening wear was closely moulded to the body, hair styles were softer, hats now had brims to them and hemlines varied between mid-calf and (in the evenings) ground-level.

Yet to appear slim was still an essential part of elegance. To this end, the

Haute Couture, 1933. The thirties emphasis on elegance and greater maturity

decade produced the suspender belt, designed to flatten the abdomen. All the styles of the years between the wars were for women with access to birth-control techniques. Birth control spread throughout the upper and middle classes, though it stopped short of the working class, where childbirth remained, for women, a perpetual disease. The

1930
'I wish you weren't so modern, Mother. It's terribly out of date.'

The contrast between the 'shocking' style of the twenties and the return to prettiness in the thirties is here clearly observed

daring minority could avoid babies before marriage; and after marriage their number was almost universally limited. These slim, gracefully athletic creatures were simply not built for frequent childbearing. Higher living standards meant that the baby had to compete with the mortgage on the new house and the hire-purchase payments on the car in the new garage. The exclusion of women from employment outside the home tended in the same direction. Outside the working class there was a steady fall in the birth-rate, and the one- or two-child family became the norm. As a result, women of all classes above the level of the unskilled workman and the unemployed neither aged as quickly as their parents and grandparents nor worked as hard as their daughters and grand-daughters, with their often larger families, their full- or part-time jobs outside the home and the absence of domestic help inside it.

More than one observer of the changing attitudes of women felt that the girls of the time were more

Hats, 1938

Glamour Glorified. Costume design by Erté for the London Palladium show, Black Velvet. *Swirling furs, pencil-slim bodies in sheath-tight dresses, with matching borzoi dog, symbolise the thirties' ideal of sophistication*

go-ahead than the young men. Male fashions reflected this relative unadventurousness. The top hat ceased to be general wear for gentlemen and salaried office workers, but it stayed for really formal occasions. It sat well, for instance, on the noble head of Ramsay MacDonald. Top hat and tails continued regulation uniform for all reputable social occasions and no sophisticated entertainer could do without them; their ultimate apotheosis as the uniform of male glamour came when Fred Astaire celebrated them in song and dance in the early thirties. Black tie and dinner-jacket, plus 'boiled shirt', a uniform known facetiously as 'soup and fish' (for example by P. G. Wodehouse's Bertie Wooster), since it was worn also by waiters at table, still indicated an informal event and not, as after 1945, an unusually formal one. It remained regulation attire for the stalls in the theatre.

Working men still wore cloth cap and choker; the bowler still bespoke the foreman, the butler off-duty and, incongruously, the Guards officer in mufti. The trilby gradually became the standard, classless headgear of the time. A trilby with a soft, wavy brim worn at an angle suggested a certain raffishness compared with one with a stiff brim. Anthony Eden rose to international acclaim with the aid of the black homburg hat, a very superior predecessor of the true trilby that harked back to the days of Edward VII. The least acceptable hat was the round 'pork-pie' version of the trilby, often in a dark green colour. Its wearer often sported a bow tie as well, and this clearly indicated a tendency to Bohemianism.

It was even a slow process securing general acceptance for

soft collars; stiffly starched white collars had a continuing life, and the type with 'butterfly wings' above the place where the tie was knotted were favoured by the Prime Ministers of the period. The only widely accepted extravagance was a result of a sudden fashion among Oxford undergraduates round about 1924 for wearing trousers with a leg-width of as much as 25 inches. These 'Oxford bags' established the fashion for wide trousers so firmly that when, 30 years later, the young reverted to narrow trousers, it appeared an unwarranted interference with an immemorial tradition. The devotion to width in the nether garment was extended to the shorts that men wore for games; professional footballers plied their skills with huge quantities of superfluous material flapping about their knees. Along with their wide flannel bags, undergraduates all wore sports jacket and pullover and for most of the time this university uniform was the most widespread form of men's leisure wear.

The other male idiosyncrasy was the grotesque and never very general long knickerbocker suit known as 'plus-fours'. Originally intended for golfers, plus-fours became so much the hall-mark of the rather fatheaded suburban young man with a desire to appear hearty and an absolute ignorance of golf that most good golfers felt compelled to wear flannels instead.

'Natty Gents' Suitings'. The plus-fours, jazzy pullover and soft collar signalise an open air occasion; but the gentleman in the stiff wing collar goes no further than to wear shoes instead of boots

By the thirties, the polo-neck sweater appeared, but only for the most informal leisure occasions. It was, however, a step in the direction of solving the problem of what a man should wear when he took his jacket off. All lounge suits had waistcoats; and though a man might take his jacket off to do rough work, he could not remove his waistcoat, since this would reveal the braces he wore to keep his trousers up; and exposed braces were 'common'. The problem was not solved until the development of self-supporting trousers which eliminated the need for braces. With this came the cellular shirt, usually referred to by the trade name of Aertex, which not only allowed the air to get to the body (or so it was said) but could be had in various pastel colours. It ended the reign of the white cricket shirt as the standard leisure shirt; to wear one of these with the shirt collar folded back over the sports-jacket collar was the sign by which the typical father would intimate that he was enjoying a day at the seaside. In the main, men's clothing, though less heavy than it had been, continued to be cumbersome and predominantly subfusc. Long woollen underpants still had adherents and the respectable working man, however mucky his workaday attire, still, when he rested on the seventh day, put on a 'Sunday suit'. It tended to be of blue serge and to be set off by brown boots.

Another prime function of the waistcoat had been to accommodate the heavy silver or gold watch and watch chain, often the most valuable of a man's personal possessions and regarded as valuable heirlooms. The twenties saw the rapid adoption of the wristwatch instead. It was disapproved of. The young man who shot out his forearm to take a studied look at this effeminately miniature timepiece, suggestive of an ornament on a lady's bracelet, was sniggered at. An affected male could for some years be crushingly condemned with the comment that he was 'terribly wristwatch' or that he 'spoke with a wristwatch accent'. The new waistcoat accessory was the fountain-pen. The names of Swan, Onoto, Waterman and then Parker replaced the names of the old steel nibs previously popularized by the advertisement that said, 'They come as a Boon and a Blessing to Men, The Pickwick, the Owl and the Waverley Pen'. Schoolmasters opposed fountain-pens on the same grounds that 30 years later they resisted ball-point pens. They would, they said, ruin their pupils' handwriting.

The overall impression created by the better-dressed men of the period was of a striving after smoothness. They shaved more of their faces and shaved them more often and successfully, perhaps because the universal adoption of the safety razor made the process less hazardous than in the days of the naked 'cut-throat' razor, which was best wielded by a professional barber. Facial hair was limited to the occasional 'natty' little moustache. This was often shaped like the bristles of a small toothbrush (and was so designated) or, owing to the influence of Clark Gable, reduced to a thin pencil's width. The hair on the head was universally short and liberally brilliantined so that it shone but lay almost flat; the ideal was never to have

Varieties of Trilby, 1926. The double-breasted lounge suit in light grey flannel was very smart

a hair out of place. When the ensemble included a lounge suit with a double-breasted jacket (with coloured silk handkerchief in breast pocket) and trousers creased to a knife-edge, the overall effect was so desperately elegant as to make men seem unrobust to the point of effeminacy. 'Young Englishmen', said a character in one of D. H. Lawrence's novels, 'all seem to me like ladies, perfect ladies.' Perhaps it was a revulsion from militarism, toughness and romantic extravagance; perhaps it was a simple consequence of the greater care for physical fitness, favouring a slim body as against a massive one, and the growing concern about personal cleanliness that characterized the whole period. Perhaps, for some, it was an innocent form of snobbery: my father worked hard at a dirty job, but I have a clean, well-paid job in an office. But the effect was as if everyone was copying the public heroes of the time by imitating their quality of slightness of physique and vulnerable youthfulness. Rupert Brooke, still greatly admired as the golden poet-martyr of the First World War, the Prince of Wales, Lindbergh the lone Atlantic flyer, the Everest climber George Mallory, and the

67

matinée idols of the London stage from Ivor Novello to the very young John Gielgud, all seemed cast in the same slimly sentimental mould.

Through all the changes of the time the Churches spoke with muted voice. Most thinking people assumed that Christianity was obsolescent, but there was a noticeable migration to Anglicanism and Romanism in the thirties by some intellectuals and towards an eclectic mysticism by others. C. S. Lewis, an Oxford English don, wrote *The Screwtape Letters* and *The Problem of Pain*, which passed for masterpieces among an intelligentsia imperfectly acquainted with theology; T. S. Eliot announced that he was Royalist, Anglican and Conservative and wrote *Murder in the Cathedral*; Aldous Huxley turned from

'*The Great Out of Doors.*' *The Men's Wear Exhibition, London, 1934. The man is wearing 'flannels with the latest elastic tops, which are worn without braces'. Observe their width. Despite the racket, the girl's outfit is 'hiking' uniform. The zip fastener was still a relative novelty; the bangles were worn on all occasions*

contemplating the sexual habits of high society to contemplation of all the world's known mystical writings with the careful exception of the Fourth Gospel; and Evelyn Waugh combined contempt for all who were not gentlemen with a staunch adherence to the Roman faith. The most notorious religious phenomenon of the thirties was the Oxford Group movement which, eventually forced to admit that its use of the word 'Oxford' was misleading, rechristened itself Moral Rearmament. An adaptation of the *Führerprinzip* to religion, it was directed from America by a Mr Frank Buchman, and lured well-heeled persons to 'house parties' where they 'shared' their sins by confessing them to all and sundry; after this, so they told everybody, they felt very happy. Bouncy, jolly, well dressed and always well connected, the Buchmanites disposed of all their critics by indicating that only sinners, atheists or crypto-Communists could possibly want to criticize them.

Although the Churches generally lost ground, the monotonous references of journalists to 'empty pews' were a little overdone. Nonconformity was perhaps less vigorous than in the past, but the Roman Church increased its proportionate membership and the Anglican Church retained a large body of the traditional-minded, except among the working classes, to whom it had never greatly appealed. Anglicanism suffered from the inadequate training of its clergy, who tended to be Oxbridge graduates or retired serving officers with a minimum of theological and almost no pastoral training. The chief Sunday services were Morning Prayer, attended by the better-off, and Evensong, favoured by those who had no servants to cook the Sunday joint for them. The very devout went (fasting) to 'the early service' (8 a.m. Communion); others 'stayed behind' on the once-monthly occasion when a truncated Communion service was tacked on to the end of Matins. The centrality of the Eucharist was propagated almost entirely by the so-called 'Anglo-Catholic' clergy (they were 'Very High Church'). Such clergymen insisted that they were priests, although most parsons of the time were reconciled to being addressed as 'padre', a practice implanted in the popular mind during the war; it suggested a decent chap who put people at their ease by not preaching at them, sometimes not wearing a dog collar and going into a pub for a drink. High Church parsons instructed their flocks that they were Catholics and not Protestants, referred to the Communion service as 'the Mass' and glorified their chancels with banners and incense and clusters of genuflecting acolytes and choristers in red cassocks. Such parsons, often in charge of unfashionable parishes, suffered surprisingly little from 'empty pews'.

The official history of the Church of England was marked by Parliament's rejection of Prayer Book Revision in 1928. On the grounds that the revisions were Romish, MPs of all sorts opposed such innovations in religion as if they were latter-day Sir John Eliots passing patriotic resolutions against the ghost of Archbishop Laud. The clergy used some of the revisions notwithstanding, particularly in the marriage service, since emancipated brides liked its omission of the wife's vow to 'obey' her husband. The only other ecclesiastical matter of public note was, first, the prolonged trial, and then the unfrocking and subsequent death in a lion's cage, of the Rev. Harold Davidson, the Rector of Stiffkey. This arose from his predilection for attempting to 'save' teenage actresses and waitresses in the more morally dangerous parts of London. Only an ecclesiastical bureaucracy as unimaginatively heavy-footed as that of the Church of England could have transformed this sadly trivial affair into a long-drawn-out *cause célèbre*.

Further Reading

Mowat, *op. cit.*, Chapter 4. Seaman, *op. cit.*, Chapter 15. A. J. P. Taylor, *England 1914–1945*, Chapter IX. Robert Graves and Alan Hodge, *The Long Week-End*, 1940, is a long-established, kaleidoscopic and all but complete account of the stunts, scandals, fashions, modes, moods, morals and crazes of the time; it flippantly supplements all chapters of this present book except Chapter X. C. W. Cunnington, *English Women's Clothes in the Present Century*, 1952, is a standard work which should be read with caution; references to what was 'the fashion' in 1928, for example, indicate what was *not* worn *before* 1928 rather than what was *generally* worn in 1928.

IV

The Pictures and the Wireless

The generation that grew up between the wars had more means of entertainment at its command than any in previous history. These years witnessed the Golden Age of the cinema, and the coming of the sound film, of colour and then the large screen; and they were also the great years of sound broadcasting.

In any list of 'significant' films, the number produced before 1930 is small, most of them the work of continental directors. Of commercial film-makers, only D. W. Griffith, Chaplin and Lubitsch did noteworthy work before the 1930s. Chaplin's most celebrated full-length productions before 1931 were *Shoulder*

Gaumont Studios, Lime Grove, London, 1922, during the shooting of the British comedy Squib Wins the Calcutta Sweep, *directed by George Pearson*

Charlie Chaplin and Jackie Coogan in The Kid, *1921*

Arms in 1918, *The Kid* (with Jackie Coogan, a small boy with bobbed hair who 'won all hearts') in 1921 and *The Gold Rush* in 1925. That few films of the 1920s had artistic value resulted from the economics and the technical limitations of the early cinema. Even then it was expensive to make films for the mass market on which they depended and they were financially profitable only if unsophisticated. Owing to the high cost, and the suspension of film-making elsewhere between 1914 and 1918, the industry was dominated by the United States. It provided 80 per cent of all the feature films shown in British cinemas which, by the 1930s, were selling as many as 20 million tickets a week.

The industry catered at the start for an audience which, though international, was without cultural standards, a characteristic they shared with film-makers themselves. The latter also had to improvise the whole art and craft of the cinema and by the end of the twenties had done so to such effect that by then the silent film was, at its best, subtle and skilful in technique. But for the mass audience an over-subtle approach was inappropriate. Situations had to be clear cut, and emotions expressed in gestures exaggerated enough to convince the least educated of minds. The cinema was, therefore, bound to exploit its chief technical novelty, its capacity to depict frenetic action, above all in the chase, whether involv-

Harold Lloyd in a characteristic predicament

ing madly careering, not-quite-colliding motor cars, galloping horses or helter-skeltering Red Indians. Its other great technical ploy was the capacity to visualize suspense and spectacular disaster. Only on the screen could heroines be rescued from the paths of oncoming express trains with barely 18 inches to spare; or motor cars hurtle over cliffs; or bad men or Indians be realistically done to death singly or in quantity; or heroes (or comedians) hang by their finger-nails to the ledges of skyscrapers; or enormous crowds rush pell-mell through burning cities; or Babylonian orgies and Roman chariot-races be stupendously re-enacted.

And so there were slapstick, knockabout, custard-pie-throwing comedies, featuring the Keystone Cops, Fatty Arbuckle, Larry Semon, Harry Langdon, Chester Conklin and cross-eyed Ben Turpin. There flourished the bespectacled, straw-hatted, bow-tied Harold Lloyd, for ever about to fall to his death and for ever just escaping it, and Buster Keaton, who asserted his individuality with a face that, whatever happened, expressed no emotion at all. Douglas Fairbanks, Senior, swung gymnastically through windows and from off balconies to rescue distressed damsels in various settings and centuries. Audiences sobbed at the terrible sufferings of Lilian Gish ('Please don't whip me,

73

Clara Bow, Hollywood sex-symbol of the early twenties

Daddy!') in *Broken Blossoms*, or thrilled to the daring deeds of Tom Mix and his white horse and the manly courage of other cowboy stars such as Dustin Farnum and W. S. Hart. There was Pola Negri, of whom it was recorded that she 'startled the world' by the 'frank realism' of her 'tempestuous characterization' of a woman 'uninhibited by conventional restraints'. There were Theda Bara, Nazimova and Clara Bow, 'vamps' with 'it' and 'oomph', wriggling their limbs, or rolling oversized eyes in ludicrous close-up. The lovesick of all ages could gush over Mary Pickford, the world's sweetheart, Valentino, the world's boyfriend, the suaver John Gilbert or the even suaver Adolphe Menjou. The selling power of Biblical spectacle to an audience many of whom were untouched by organized religion, was exploited in technical masterpieces of remarkable aesthetic

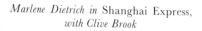

Marlene Dietrich in Shanghai Express, *with Clive Brook*

vulgarity, such as *The Four Horsemen of the Apocalypse* and the silent versions of *The Ten Commandments*, *The King of Kings* and *Ben Hur*.

The coming of sound, from 1928 onwards, led at first to deterioration. Many experienced silent stars had unusable voices, and the inevitably infantile reaction of the human being to a novel gadget produced concentration on cinematized speech and song without regard for film structure. The conjunction of spectacle with popular music ('The Talkies' were advertised as 'All Talking, All Singing, All Dancing') was also predictable, and the thirties were preeminently the years of spectacular American musicals with enormous casts

of sweet-faced leggy girls appearing to sing their hearts out while executing energetic arabesques in the lushest of surroundings, and wearing elaborately feathered headgear. The association these musicals achieved between the talents of song-writers such as Jerome Kern and Cole Porter and the dancing feet of Fred Astaire, with his succession of lissom dancing partners (of whom Ginger Rogers was but one) or the relaxed, good-natured skill of Bing Crosby, brought more pleasure to more people in a few short years than anything before in history.

The coming of sound transferred to the cinema rather more of the sophisticated style of acting which the 1920s had brought to the stage. It proved a boon to Greta Garbo, whose subtlety had made her outstanding on the silent screen; the less physically hectic technique of the sound film was particularly suited to her.

English films and English actors also benefited from the change. Stiff-upper-lipped Englishmen like Clive Brook, Herbert Marshall and above all Ronald Colman came into their own. Englishmen could provide panache, too. Charles Laughton's performances in *The Private Life of Henry VIII* (1934) and *Rembrandt* (1936)—both British films—were outstanding. Hardly less successful British films were *Pygmalion* with Leslie Howard and *The Citadel* with Robert Donat. The 1930s also saw the rise of Hitchcock as a director, with such films as *Secret Agent*, *Saboteur* and *The Lady Vanishes*.

Greta Garbo as Queen Christina, with John Gilbert

Charles Laughton in The Private Life of Henry VIII, *with Binnie Barnes, a British feature film directed by Sir Alexander Korda*

Apart from Chaplin's full-length satire on the Machine Age, *Modern Times*, the old comic tradition was chiefly carried on into sound by Laurel and Hardy, but the coming divorce between comedy and pathos was foreshadowed by the emergence of the Marx Brothers; unlike Chaplin with his concern for society's lost sheep, or Stan Laurel, brought near to tears by his own helpless incompetence, or Oliver Hardy, so coyly courteous and courtly, the Marx Brothers were amoral anarchists. The old cowboy films changed, too; they became Westerns, and highbrows said they liked them because of the scenery (particularly when colour came in) and the simple morality they taught. Uglier violence shifted to gangster films.

Cartoon films preceded sound. Two crude figures, one tall and the other short, called Mutt and Jeff, were for a short while household words. More endearing was Felix the Cat, whose adventures were representatively described in song:

> *Felix keeps on walking*
> *Keeps on walking still*
> *With his hands behind him*
> *You will surely find him.*
> *They blew him up with dynamite*
> *But him they couldn't kill*
> *Miles up in the air he flew*
> *He just murmured toodle-oo*
> *Landed down in Timbuctoo*
> *And keeps on walking still.*

With the appearance of Mickey Mouse in 1929, Disney came into his own. Mickey Mouse, Donald Duck, Pluto and the Three Little Pigs ('Who's Afraid of the Big Bad Wolf?') were almost as real as the human stars of the 1930s; and Disney's first full-length feature, *Snow White and the Seven Dwarfs*, appeared in 1938. Those who liked sentimentality without Disney's admixture of vulgarity, brutality and ugliness, could admire instead the curls and dimples of the child star, Shirley Temple, the noble deeds of the Alsatian doggy star, Rin Tin Tin, for ever rescuing men, women and children from catastrophe, or the endearing charms of the very young Judy Garland and Micky Rooney.

76

'Stupendous Spectacle'. Claudette Colbert as Cleopatra, 1934

The most painful aspect of cinema-going in the 1930s was the
cinema organ, almost always described as 'The Mighty Wurlitzer', which was a feature of most of the big cinemas. By a
miraculous engineering feat, the console was made to rise slowly
from the depths to the level of the stage, while soft, ever-
changing, ever-mingling coloured lights bathed the organist
and the closed curtains with a moody effulgence. He played
popular tunes (with 'effects') and 'rendered' such 'old favourites'
as 'Love's Old Sweet Song' or Ketelbey's 'In a Monastery
Garden' or (and here the effects with bells were delightful) 'In
a Persian Market'. His recital over, organist and console sank
down into the underworld again, to thunders of applause.

The Mighty Wurlitzer was the hall-mark of the 'super-
cinemas' of the thirties. Originally, cinemas had tried to commend themselves as 'picture palaces' but by 1930 this had come
to indicate a place that was little better than a 'fleapit' (a word
perhaps indicative of working-class living standards in the early
part of the century). Super-cinemas were big enough to seat up
to 3,000 'patrons' and were glorified with names appropriate to
a decade obsessed with 'glamour' such as Ritz, Majestic, Rialto,

'Plush cathedrals of pleasure.' Interior of the Granada Cinema, Tooting, London, with the console of the 'mighty organ' raised up in the effulgent light

Roxy, Astoria, Granada, State. They were the cathedrals of their day, devoted to the silent decorous worship of the Great Stars and so crammed with the Faithful that by early evening the superbly uniformed commissionaires were already intoning to the patient, queueing crowds, 'Seats at 2s. 4d. only, standing at 8d. and 1s. 3d.' One passed through the 'foyer' and up the grand, richly carpeted staircase, with stills showing the Stars of movies past or 'Coming Shortly', like a pagan epoch's substitute for the icons of Byzantium, to be conducted to one's 'fauteuil' by an attendant maiden, now for the first time being called an 'usherette', who later, when the Mighty Wurlitzer played, would supply the new, hygienically wrapped ice-cream bricks or the even more novel 'choc-ice'. The 'décor' of the super-cinema would be Millionaire's Baroque: cherubs, cornucopias, and flambeaux of coloured glass to diffuse the concealed light-ing, which was one of various contemporary ways of proving it was possible to be both very modern and very tasteful at one and the same time.

The speedy triumph of the cinema habit is easily explained. It was so cheap that, in the 1930s, it was possible to have three hours' entertainment (at special matinée prices) for 6d. or 8d. on any afternoon before tea-time. Performances were continuous, thus eliminating the booking rituals of the theatre. One could

78

go at a time to suit oneself or even on the spur of the moment. The seats were comfortable, which was true neither of the theatre, the music-hall nor the local church. Even for the best seats, one did not have to dress up: in contrast to the theatre, the only person wearing evening dress in the average cinema would be the manager. The cinema was warm and, again unlike the theatre, though gregarious, a place of private pleasure; and since warmth and privacy were rarities in working-class homes the unemployed could resort to the cinema for warmth and courting couples go there for privacy.

The lower orders were continually berated by their betters for their addiction to celluloid artifice, and it was taken for granted that the minds of the young would be corrupted and their ideas distorted by what they saw on the screen. These criticisms were no better than the attitude of the old-fashioned parent condemning a child for 'always having his head stuck in a book'; and the working-class young were perfectly capable of realizing that the world of the film star was one of make-believe. The cinema did not, for such people, take the place of more enriching pastimes, since opportunities for these hardly existed. The cinema added to experience; it did not subtract from it. It kept the young off the aimless streets and their elders out of the pubs; and these, in the industrial towns, were the real alternatives. The cinema represented the first major cultural victory of the people of the working classes over their middle-class betters; a revolutionary art form created by and for the people of the back streets had conquered the world, with Kennington-born Charlie Chaplin's little man as its entirely appropriate trail-blazer.

While the cinema was condemned for being vulgar, broadcasting in England was criticized for being narrowly middle class. The British Broadcasting Company was founded in 1922, and in 1926 transformed into the first major public corporation, the British Broadcasting Corporation. There were technical reasons for establishing a monopoly in broadcasting and vesting it in a body which, though independent of Government, was ultimately responsible to a Minister of the Crown (the Postmaster-General); but an additional factor was the vigorously

The Radio Times *is born, 28 September 1923*

expressed idealism of J. C. W. Reith (later Sir John, and then Lord, Reith). Reith was Managing Director of the Company and then Director-General of the Corporation until 1938. He insisted that broadcasting should be a public service, that it should have definite standards and should not merely entertain but also edify. Reith maintained this tradition so persistently that it outlasted him. The English owed much to Reith, with his Late Victorian earnestness and sense of mission. He enabled them to enjoy sound radio without the intrusion of commercial advertising; he provided opportunities for cultural and musical self-education to many who might otherwise have lacked them; and, by resisting an attempt by Baldwin's Government to secure Government control of news during the General Strike, he established standards of integrity and independence in the presentation of news and current affairs higher than those prevailing among other media and in other countries at the time.

National occasion. Trumpeters broadcast The Last Post from 2LO, London, on Armistice Day, 1923

Listening to the wireless was an arduous business to begin with: a matter of crystal sets, cat's-whiskers, ear-phones and long, high roof-top aerials. A door hastily slammed would disrupt everything by dislodging the cat's whiskers; an absent-minded decision by a head-phone wearer to move across the room would bring the apparatus crashing to the floor. This was soon remedied by the coming of the valve set, atop which a loudspeaker reared up like the horn of the gramophones of the time; and to have a four- or six-valve wireless set was like having, years later, a car with twin carburettors. In the early days, handymen constructed their sets themselves, using circuits printed in specialist magazines, such as *Popular Wireless*; but by the 1930s wireless sets could be pieces of furniture, hardly less impressive than that other feature of the 'posh' suburban home, the cocktail cabinet. Sets were large (because not transistorized and because the built-in speakers were large) and were sometimes allied with a built-in turntable to form the radiogram. It thus became possible to listen to the dinner-plate '78s' of the time without the repeated winding of clockwork mechanism; and many radiograms had automatic record-changers. Such massive pieces of machinery were beyond the purses of ordinary folk, however.

Sir John Reith, Director General of the BBC, addresses a conference on Wireless and Adult Education, 1932. Lapel-gripping was a customary oratorical device of the period

At first, the mere wonder of the wireless was enough; and thousands several times sat up into the small hours to hear a lady 'cellist coax a nightingale into song on the Surrey hills. Very soon, however, the BBC settled down to become a middle-brow university of the air. Sir Walford Davies, the Master of the King's Musick, gave avuncular talks on the rudiments of musical theory and Percy Scholes, compiler of the *Oxford Companion to Music*, spoke feelingly about singers who were guilty of a lot of *tremolo*. Desmond MacCarthy, the urbane literary critic, talked regularly on books; James Agate, the mannered drama critic of the *Sunday Times*, reviewed plays, and there were even film reviews. Intelligent reviewing of gramophone records began with Christopher Stone, sometimes referred to as the first disc-jockey, though this does him less than justice. Cyril Burt talked on psychology: there were talks by Beatrice

Webb, Bernard Shaw and G. K. Chesterton. This cultural emphasis shifted in the 1930s to informed if rather despairingly liberal comment on international affairs by men such as Vernon Bartlett and Stephen King-Hall. An evening-class lecturer on horticulture achieved national fame by broadcasting talks on gardening and was perhaps the last radio celebrity to be spoken of as 'Mr'—he was always 'Mr Middleton'.

For the popularization of music the BBC did much. It ran a long series in the 1920s called the 'Foundations of Music', which provoked sarcastic comment; it broadcast opera; it took over the sponsoring of the Promenade Concerts in Henry Wood's hey-day and created the BBC Symphony Orchestra under Adrian Boult. It did little for modern or experimental music, but criticism on this score came from persons already musically educated and able to go to London concerts; the great need of the time was to popularize standard works among people with little musical knowledge and no access to concert halls. It devoted a high proportion of its efforts in early days to encouraging the listening habit among the young with its 45-minute Children's Hour: the mood was nice, kindly, and unvulgar. Children's Hour, too, was criticized as too middle class, but this simply meant that it treated children as potentially intelligent beings and not as mere fodder for the entertainment industry. The first radio play occurred in Children's Hour, and the 'Toytown' series of plays ran for years, making Larry the Lamb and Mr Grouser ('It's *disgraceful*, sir!') rivals in the nicer households of the land to Mickey Mouse and Donald Duck. The doyen of Children's Hour 'uncles' was Derek McCulloch, an extremely sympathetic personality who kept children's radio civilized and unpatronizing.

Under Val Gielgud and Tyrone Guthrie, radio drama achieved a fine professional competence, with a general level of performance superior to that of the legitimate stage at the time. But what the BBC loved best was the Outside Broadcast of the Great National Occasion. In the 1930s, Christmas Day was the occasion for an elaborate Empire-wide Round-up, with messages from people in all walks of life from as many remote corners of the Empire as possible, all culminating promptly at

3 p.m. in a message 'to all my people everywhere' broadcast, live, by King George V. His words came out slowly and carefully, paternally and benevolently, and in a slightly guttural voice that gave him a highly appropriate classlessness. The BBC was always in trouble about its so-called 'BBC accent'. Common people thought it posh and superior people said it would annihilate regional speech in favour of colourless uniformity. This was as if, in the sixteenth century, people had opposed the printing of books on the grounds that it would lead to standardized spelling. In fact, the sensation of one of the BBC's splendid Christmas Round-ups was an anonymous 'old shepherd of the Cotswolds' whose rustic accents stole the whole Imperial show so thoroughly that it is tempting to regard him as the true original of that much later BBC creation, Dan Archer.

The BBC likewise disseminated popular music, though it preferred not to risk contumely by broadcasting anything that jazzmen would call 'real' jazz. Regular late-evening broadcasts of the Savoy Orpheans dance band from the Savoy Hotel, London, was the first big step in the social revolution by which the amusements of the few and rich were made in some measure accessible to the impecunious many ('Roll up your carpet and dance at home to the finest dance band in London'). The early evening was enlivened (perhaps to give the illusion of participating in a smart 'tea dance') by a 'resident' band: Sidney Firman and the London Radio Dance Band was succeeded by Jack Payne and his Band and then by the long-surviving Henry Hall and his BBC Dance Orchestra. Comedy and 'Variety' were not neglected, though long tending to be insipid. André Charlot, the West End impresario whose revues were a vehicle for the talents of Noel Coward and Gertrude Lawrence, produced milder versions of these revues for radio. The first BBC comic was a lugubrious Yorkshireman called John Henry, gloomily telling of his henpecked sufferings at the hands of his wife, Blossom. Regular favourites were the cross-talk comedians, Clapham and Dwyer, who once fell from grace by letting slip the word 'Damn'. They were sharply rebuked by authority and when next they broadcast they repeatedly referred to two famous Dutch cities as 'Rotter' and 'Amster'. They would not,

'Big-hearted' Arthur Askey and Richard 'Stinker' Murdoch in a broadcast of Band Waggon, *1938. The microphone has changed greatly since 1923*

they said, risk further trouble by uttering the names in full. The most effective wireless comedian from the earliest days was Tommy Handley, though he did not become a national institution till the days of 'Itma' during the Second World War. He poured endless verbal nonsense into the microphone and at such a rate that the cumulative effect was much greater than that of any of the individual parts. He had an astonishing facility for bubbling comicality without recourse to the vulgar or the suggestive. In the last years of the period came the first of the successful comedy series, 'Band Waggon', with Arthur Askey and Richard Murdoch. Askey's catchphrase 'Aythankyiaow', though no more than a reproduction of what London bus conductors had been saying for years as they punched out bus tickets with their bell punches, passed into nationwide usage.

Most open to criticism was the BBC's obsession with religious broadcasting. This derived from Reith's own deeply felt convictions and caused it to be alleged that he always asked an applicant for employment in the BBC if he believed in Jesus Christ. Although certainly intended to Keep Britain Christian, it is possible that the daily services, and the morning and evening services and late-night epilogues on Sundays, and the devotional talks for every season of the Christian year gave many people an excuse for not going to church at all; one got better music and just as good sermons by stopping at home, even on Sunday. BBC religion was careful, moderate and bland. The only personality to escape from this cocoon of pious correctitude was Canon H. R. L. Sheppard, Vicar of St Martin's-in-the Fields, London. His broadcast sermons were unclerically conversational, masculine without heartiness and

84

A 'Baird Cathode Ray TV Receiver' being demonstrated in London, 1935. It receives Mickey Mouse on a tiny screen

though sentimental not effusive. His unorthodoxy was expressed more thoroughly in the 1930s by his strong support of pacifism; but by that time he no longer broadcast. The BBC's Puritanism caused many to listen, particularly on Sundays, to Radio Luxembourg, which broadcast programmes of commercially sponsored popular music. The jingle that indicated the sponsorship of a well-known milk drink ('We are the Ovalteenies') was a universal favourite.

On 2 November 1936 the BBC opened its television service, from Alexandra Palace, London. Although in 1939 there were still only 50,000 viewers, and transmission then ceased until after 1945, the coming of television was a portent. In the 1920s and 1930s the cinema and sound radio swept all before them. By the 1950s, cinemas were closing down at the rate of four every week and sound broadcasting programmes appeared in the newspapers in small print, almost as footnotes to the more boldly displayed announcement of the day's television.

Further Reading

Roger Manvell, *Film*, 1944, though a classic on the cinema, is mainly a guide to what intellectuals thought films ought to be like and says little about the films people actually saw. A more general survey may be found in Paul Rotha, *The Film Till Now*, various editions from 1930 to 1967. For the memoirs of a British film director whose association with films in this country lasted from 1913 to 1955 see George Pearson, *Flashback*, 1957. Asa Briggs, *History of Broadcasting in the United Kingdom*, volumes I and II, 1961–5, is large and reverential and, therefore, a useful antidote to the carping attitude taken to the BBC by intellectual writers and perpetuated by Taylor, *op. cit.*, pages 233–4 and 307.

V

Say It With Music

The effect of the gramophone, the wireless and, after 1928, the sound film, was to enable people of all classes to hear, in a week, more music, and more varied music, than their ancestors might have heard in a lifetime. Much of the music disseminated in this way was regarded as shockingly different from both 'serious' music and the popular music of the past.

This difference is often expressed by referring to the 1920s as 'the Jazz Age'; the starting-point of this in England is held to be the arrival in London of the Original Dixieland Jazzband in 1919. In practice, however, jazz continued for the most part to be the music of coloured Americans (the Dixieland Jazzband performers were white) gravitating from New Orleans to the speakeasies of Chicago and Kansas City and the bars and theatres of New York; almost from the beginning the knowledgeable minority made a sharp distinction between this 'real' jazz and the 'commercial' jazz of the entertainment industry. This did not prevent almost all popular music of the 1920s being indiscriminately labelled 'jazz' and condemned as negroid and therefore uncivilized. Aldous Huxley confidently declared, 'Modern popular music is more barbarous than any folk art has been, at any rate in Western Europe, for hundreds of years.' The Editor of the *Oxford History of Music*, Sir Henry Hadow, having heard 'an expensive jazzband in America,' reported in 1927, 'the players were extremely skilful; the pieces were without any structural interest, the harmonies were like a cheap oleograph and the melodic invention was in rags'. Even Constant Lambert could be no more sympathetic than to describe jazz as a combination of Debussy and *Hymns, Ancient*

An Era Begins: the Original Dixieland Jazz Band at the Hammersmith Palais de Danse, 1919

and Modern; and not until the days of rock-'n'-roll did a musical fashion excite such general disapproval.

If the popular music of the period was not 'real' jazz, it was certainly jazzy. It copied the jazz emphasis on the off-beat and the jazz technique of using (or misusing) brass and reed instruments to imitate the human voice, which gave rise to the sounds expressed vocally as 'do-wack-a-do' or 'boop-a-doop' and 'vo-de-o-do'. It reproduced the staccato, jerky jolliness of the Dixieland style, and, though in fairly genteel fashion, the brooding melancholy of the Blues; and there was much talk later on about 'swing', though there was universal agreement that nobody could define swing, but only recognize it when they heard it. The comic, extrovert qualities of early jazz were widely copied, so that, for the young at any rate, music and music-making became something uproarious and unpretentious. The least successful borrowing was the vocal; though white performers could make tolerable jazz instrumentalists they made such inferior jazz vocalists that they took to 'crooning' instead; and except when done by Bing Crosby in his prime or by England's own favourite, Al Bowlly, crooning tended to be a polite word for moaning. Popular music benefited most from the encouragement that jazz gave to extemporization and to the individual soloist. 'Real' jazzmen often created hit tunes or transformed existing ones, and it is because of this that the hit

Al Bowlly, prince of England's crooners

tunes of the time showed a capacity for survival which made nonsense of the contemporary condemnation of them as purely ephemeral. They were given fresh life again and again by successive interpreters, arrangers and orchestras, and still honoured, 30 or 40 years after their emergence, as 'standards' or 'oldies' and liable once in a while, in transmogrified form, to appear in the 'charts' of the sixties.

The predominant influence was inevitably American. All through the 1920s the English young sang songs designed to express the nostalgia of first-generation American city-dwellers for the old folks at home. English children and young persons sang 'Swanee' ('How I love you, my dear old Swanee'), affirmed a desire to be 'Back Home in Tennessee' ('I'll see my sweetheart Flo and friends I used to know') or to return to 'Omaha' ('I'm a comin' back to you'). They declared that they were 'Alabammy bound' and asserted that nothing could be finer than to 'Be in Carolina' or besought the moon in those parts to keep on 'shining on the one who waits for me'. They extolled the beauties of 'Twilight on Missouri' or of any time of day in 'Pasadena'; and summed it all up in that most nostalgic of all their songs of alienation, 'Bye Bye Blackbird' ('No one here can love or understand me'). They sang light-hearted songs like 'Singing in the Rain' and 'Blue Skies', strenuously cheerful ones like

> *Stand on both your legs*
> *Be like two fried eggs*
> *Keep Your Sunny Side Up!*

and yearning ones like 'What'll I Do?' ('When you are far away and I am blue, What'll I do?'), 'I've Got You Under My Skin' and that most admired of Gershwin's songs, 'The Man I Love'. They sang ridiculous songs like 'Horsey, Keep Your Tail Up' and 'Yes! We have No Bananas' or 'All By Yourself in the

Moonlight' and 'I'm One of the Nuts of Barcelona'. They sang, particularly in the 1920s, coyly innocent songs, of which 'Tea for Two' the hit tune from *No, No, Nanette* was for ever un-rivalled in its wholly infectious banality:

> *Tea for Two and Two for Tea*
> *Just Me for You and You for Me Alone. . . .*
> *Day Will Break and You'll Awake*
> *And Start to Bake a Sugar Cake*
> *For Me to Take for All the Boys to See*
> *We will Raise a Family*
> *A Boy for You a Girl for Me*
> *Oh can't you See How Happy We Will Be!*

Not all these songs were American; but, in challenge to America's Gershwin, Irving Berlin, Rodgers and Hart, Jerome Kern and Cole Porter, England could offer only Horatio Nicholls, Ray Noble and Noel Gay. Of jazz-type orchestras, apart from the BBC's Jack Payne and Henry Hall, there were Jack Hylton, Fred Elizalde, Lew Stone, Ambrose, Roy Fox and Geraldo; but the name of Paul Whiteman, the American band leader, rather exaggeratedly known as 'The King of Jazz', nevertheless outshone them all. The English speciality was rather in revue, where the jazz influence tinkled rather than clattered. Thus, the East End of London's Limehouse district, with its Chinese element, was made to do service as an English equivalent of New York's Har-lem and the song 'Limehouse Blues', as sung by England's Gertrude Lawrence, achieved

Yes! We Have No Bananas—*the nonsense song that swept the country in 1923. The popularity of a song was then measured by the number of copies of sheet music sold*

Nº 1462.
6ᵈ EDITION
ELLIS·COLLECTON·ASHTON
The Sensational Comedy Song Fox-Trot

YES! WE HAVE NO BANANAS

ELLIS·COLLECTON·ASHTON

COMEDY SONG FOX-TROT.

Words and Music
by

FRANK SILVER
and IRVING COHN.

Copyright.
Price 6ᵈ net
LAWRENCE WRIGHT MUSIC Cº
Denmark Street (Charing Cross Rd)
LONDON. W.C.2.

HORATIO NICHOLLS BALLADS

(Printed in England)

'Star'. The frail-voiced Gertrude Lawrence, admired on both sides of the Atlantic

Jack Buchanan, elegant tap dancing star of revue, stage and screen

fame on both sides of the Atlantic. Gershwin returned the compliment by writing 'Someone to Watch Over Me' specially to suit Gertrude Lawrence's fragile, uncertain singing style. Ivor Novello wrote sophisticated songs such as 'And Her Mother Came Too' for the elegantly tap-dancing Jack Buchanan, whose singing voice was hardly more robust than Gertrude Lawrence's. Coward composed songs which were both of the Jazz Age and a comment upon it, like 'Mad About the Boy' and 'Poor Little Rich Girl'. All these songs and performers were acclaimed in America. The thirties produced a few English musical films with memorable songs: Anna Neagle and Jack Buchanan sang 'Good Night Vienna' with such success that by the end of the decade Miss Neagle had soared to the heights of representing Queen Victoria on stage and screen in *Sixty Glorious Years*; and Jessie Matthews (30 years later to become BBC radio's last Mrs Dale) sang the Rodgers and Hart number 'Dancing on the Ceiling' and danced memorably to it in *Evergreen*.

The brevity of their original existence in the 'hit parade' (they all had to die a little before being resurrected) and their sheer multiplicity combined to give to the tunes of the time a personal, evocative quality more precise than that possessed by earlier music. Two phrases of the time point to this fact: 'Darling, they're playing *our* tune' (which soon became a joke) and the

Noel Coward line, 'How potent cheap music is'. Earlier songs could recall a period, a climate of feeling, a half-forgotten way of life. The hits of the 1920s and 1930s often attracted to themselves the associations of a particular month or week or even of a particular place at a particular moment. They could re-create forgotten sensations with such immediacy that the discovery of lost time which Proust took 12 long volumes to arrive at could be experienced by the most ordinary minds whenever a song of last year or the year before came drifting back into the idle brain, or whenever someone casually put a record on the gramophone.

The older musical tradition of frontally assaulting the more vulnerable emotions also flourished, hardly touched by jazz influences, in such musical shows as *The Maid of the Mountains* ('where hearts are true and skies are blue'), *Rose Marie*, *The Desert Song* and *The Vagabond King*, in which a male chorus of 'sons of toil' worked themselves into a lather of patriotic excitement on behalf of the King of France culminating in the tremendous pay-off line 'And to HELL with Burgundee!' A continental flavour returned in the thirties. *The White Horse Inn* started a fashion for dirndl skirts; and *Lilac Time*, which was all about Schubert, started a fashion for its accomplished German tenor lead, Richard Tauber; so much so that one newspaper humorist averred that Schubert's last words had been 'Don't

Jessie Matthews, with trilling voice, long-legged dancing and a spice of Cockney impudence, in Evergreen

Noel Coward in 1935

91

A Crossword Puzzle 'Novelty' Dance in progress at the Palais de Danse in East Ham, to the east of London, 1925. No very young people are visible; most of the dancers are in ordinary walking shoes

let poor Tauber starve.' Tauber singing, with Teutonic accent, a song called 'You Are My Heart's Delight' was almost a permanent feature of life in England in the thirties.

All these were outshone by native talent. Coward's *Bitter Sweet* provided sopranos for years to come with 'I'll See You Again' and Ivor Novello's *Glamorous Night* and *The Dancing Years* poured out a prodigal wealth of lilting sentimental melody against a background of romantic Ruritanian splendour and heartbreak. Yet the thirties ended with the wildly successful *Me and My Girl*, containing an allegedly cockney song and dance called 'Doing the Lambeth Walk' at whose conclusion everybody had to say 'Oi!' *Me and My Girl* was totally unrelated to anything that had happened in the field of popular entertainment during the previous 20 years and came as a startling reminder that even as late as 1938–9 a large num-

Dance Band, 1932. The Blue River Boys at the Hotel de Paris. The svelte appearance and well brilliantined hair were characteristic. The brown and white shoes were considered rather 'flashy'

ber of ordinary English people still wished they could be 'Down at the Old Bull and Bush' with their grandmothers.

The Tango, demonstrated by experts, 1925

All this music, the jazzily jolly, the insidiously crooned or the liltingly melodious, was everywhere available, providing a mass culture that was coming to be a classless culture. The wireless disseminated it, the gramophone perpetuated it and in drill halls, church halls, social clubs, men's institutes and in commercial dance halls (the most ambitious of which would be called a 'Palais de Danse') dance bands of every degree of proficiency played it to minister to the national pastime of dancing. This could be enjoyed in the smartest London hotels and at the other end of the scale at a shilling 'hop' in a provincial Scout hut with wooden walls, a corrugated-iron roof and a brief speech of embarrassed bonhomie by the local vicar. The needs of the nation's dancers called into existence innumerable small dance bands manned by young, part-time musicians who had learned to play saxophone, trumpet or drums, thus early refuting the charge that the young could no longer make music by themselves. The favourite dances were the fox-trot, the one-step and an unathletic version of the waltz. The celebrated Charleston was more of a joke than a nationally successful dance and the 'black bottom' hardly got further than the newspaper headlines. The tango fared better, though it was regarded as a bit showy. As Beverley Nichols wrote of it later, 'as performed in those days it gave the illusion that the participants were threading their way along the ledges of dangerous precipices . . . and the arms were spread out stiffly groping, as it were, at the walls of imaginary cliffs'. In the main, the average dance-hall atmosphere was solemn and sedate, with each couple wholly absorbed in each other. Extravagant activity of any sort was usually ruled out by lack of space. There was little of the boisterous extrovert formation dancing of the old sort (though the veleta usually appeared once during the evening) or of the exuberant individualism of the dances of the future. Jitterbugging, which crept in in the face of much disapproval at the end of the 1930s, pointed the way to that future.

The part played by the gramophone was increased with the development of electrical recording and the sale of cheap six-inch 'singles' for sixpence at Woolworth's, where the assistants made sure they were constantly being played. Gramophones were still bulky and clumsy, though the trumpet had now gone; the sound-box and the steel needle had not yet completely given way to the electrical pick-up and the connoisseur's best alternative to the steel needle was one made of hard fibre; a variety of gadgets was devised for sharpening these fibre needles. And since the best reproduction was via a radiogram, the youthful cult of obsessed private listening to records had little chance to develop between the wars. The gramophone, like the wireless set, was a family possession in the way the television set was in the 1950s and 1960s; and the tastes of the young were less dominant.

The success of *Me and My Girl* in 1938 is a reminder that the claim that the cinema killed the old music-hall is exaggerated. Many music-halls became cinemas; but a number survived in the larger industrial towns and in London. So did music-hall performers, though they came to be referred to as 'variety artistes'. They did the rounds of the surviving halls, turned up at the seaside for the summer and did an annual stint in pantomime; and their number was replenished by newcomers who, like their elders, found new opportunities in radio and also in the cinemas which, in the 1930s, often included live 'variety' interludes. Of the older generation, the raddled vulgarian, Nellie Wallace, with her tipsy hats, long survived. So did Gertie Gitana, singing 'Nellie Dean', G. H. Elliot, the 'chocolate coloured coon', Harry Tate with a ragingly irascible motoring sketch, Billy Bennett, red nosed and coarse but 'Almost a Gentleman', Ella Shields, the male impersonator ('I'm Burlington Bertie') and Kate Carney singing 'Are we to part like this, Bill' with most moving dignity. Charlie Coburn, who had sung 'Two Lovely Black Eyes' and 'The Man Who Broke the Bank at Monte Carlo', emerged to sing them all over again on the wireless in the late 1930s, and Randolph Sutton, billed as 'England's Premier Light Comedian', sang 'On Mother Kelly's Doorstep' for something like 40 years. Northern audiences were devoted to Frank Randle, an earthy Lancashire comic who portrayed an alcoholic and bawdily amorous hiker, and to Norman Evans who, since he was not quite so fundamental as Frank Randle, received the accolade of a summons to a Royal Command performance. There were others, more widely celebrated. Even Tommy Handley toured the halls in the early 1920s with a knock-about army sketch called 'The Disorderly Room'. George Formby, Junior, was well within the tradition with his 'I'm Leaning on a Lamp-post on the Corner of the Street' ('in case a certain Little Lady passes by') and his Chinese laundryman, Mr Wu ('He's got a

'Cheeky Chappie', Max Miller. The jokes were blue, the costume vulgar, the timing superb, the audience-control complete

naughty eye that flickers/When he's ironing ladies' blouses'), and so was Will Hay, as a bizarre schoolmaster with a supporting cast of idiot pupils. Flanagan and Allen as a down-and-out couple singing 'Underneath the Arches' were wholly of the old music-hall, as was Max Miller as the 'Cheeky Chappie' with wide plus-fours, his leering suggestiveness ('No, you got me wrong, lady') and his shady salesman-like patter whose style was to be heard in real life among the sellers of cheap china and lace curtains in all the urban street markets of the time.

Gracie Fields was the one performer in the tradition to commend herself to all classes. Highbrows sentimentalized about

'Our Gracie' in a scene from the British film Sally. *Her high, carrying voice and Lancashire accent always retained echoes of a mill girl making herself heard above the clattering weaving machines of her native Rochdale*

her on the grounds that she was 'authentic' and clergymen praised her for being 'healthy'. She had bouncing vitality, comprehensive good nature, and a Lancashire accent whose bright freshness in an entertainment industry already given over to a mid-Atlantic nasal proclaimed that she was not only a child of Rochdale but the jolly daughter of every old-fashioned, jolly English father in the land. She had a strange falsetto singing voice which she exploited to the full for comic effect, and conformed to tradition by drawing her material from the domestic life of the industrial working class and by combining comedy with sentimentality, including religious sentimentality. Her songs were concerned with 'Granny's Little Old Skin Rug' and 'The Biggest Aspidistra in the World' and love-shy young men ('Walter, Walter, Lead me to the Altar'). Her signature tune (as the new phrase had it) was a song called 'Sally' ('Pride of Our Alley') which perhaps reminded her audience of the much older song 'Sally in our Alley' which they probably learned in singing lessons at their elementary schools. Her tear-jerkers included 'Little Old Lady Passing By' since songs about mothers and old ladies were a music-hall stand-by; and then, the audience having been thoroughly softened up, her conclusion was likely to be Schubert's 'Ave Maria', to which her high sexless voice was not unsuited. Her only rival in this speciality was a Master Ernest Lough, a choirboy whose record of 'Oh for the Wings of a Dove' was a best-seller.

The over-forties liked Our Gracie rather better than did the under-thirties, but the over-forties were in general impervious to all but the most sentimental of the hit tunes. Wherever the urban masses congregated for a sing-song, in the local on Saturday night or in a pub on a by-pass on the way home from a day trip by charabanc to Blackpool or Southend, they sang the songs of the years before 1918. Those most commonly sung in a state of alcoholic euphoria were 'Dear Old Pals' ('DEAR ole pals, JOLLY ole pals, Give me the FRIEN'ship of DEAR ole pals'), 'Nellie Dean' ('There's an old mill by the stream, Nellie Dean') and 'Lily of Laguna', which it was sad indeed to hear raucously droned out by swaying figures soggy with mild and bitter, since it was a tenderly meditative song in its original conception. For more sober moments, the working-class over-forties still clung to very old favourites, strongly concerned with marital affection, such as 'Because' ('Because God made thee mine, I cherish thee and Hold your Hand for All Eternity'). They mourned a departed loved one ('Speak, speak, speak to me Thora, Speak from your Heaven to me', and 'If Those Lips Could Only Speak'). They sang 'Kind, Kind and Gentle is She, Kind is My Mary' or expressed most movingly the old longing for lost rural felicities: 'I'll take you home again, Kathleen / To where your heart will feel no Pain / To where the fields are Fresh and Green / I will Take You Home Again'. The survival of these firmly constructed, strongly emotional ballads was a constant reminder of how new and different was the post-1918 world, where it was possible to visualize matrimony in the tinklingly trivial manner of the lovers of *No, No, Nanette*. But it was also an object-lesson instructing the observer that amid all that was new in those years, old ways and old ideas had lost surprisingly little of their hold.

Further Reading (and listening)

E. Short, *Fifty Years of Vaudeville, 1894–1945*, deals with the music-hall. Beverley Nichols, *Sweet and Twenties*, 1958, has much affectionate gossip about songs, and Chapter XXVI of his *Twenty-Five*, 1926, ('Containing the Hideous Truth about Noel Coward') is a many-treasured period piece. Richard Hoggart, *Uses of Literacy*, 1957, refers to many of the 'good old songs' still being sung in the interwar period and afterwards. *Jazz in Perspective*, BBC Publications, 1969, is a beginner's introduction to the 'real' jazz of the period. A basic discography might start with *My Baby Loves to Charleston*, MFP 1158, for the twenties, *Vic Dickensen Showcase*, FJL 404, for mainstream jazz of the thirties, and *The Incomparable Gertrude Lawrence*, ACL 1171 which reveals that she did not sing at all like Miss Julie Andrews. Characteristic songs of the whole period from *No, No, Nanette* onwards are sung by Binnie Hale on WRC SH 129 (*Spread a Little Happiness*).

VI

Increasingly to School

The State-education system between the wars was based on the Education Act of 1870 which had established elementary schools, the Act of 1902 which created State secondary schools and the 1918 Act which raised the school-leaving age to 14. Elementary schools catered for children from five to 14 and the maintained and aided secondary schools (called, after 1944, 'secondary grammar schools') served the highly intelligent minority and also the moderately intelligent, provided their parents could afford the fees of from three to five guineas a term. Since the County Councils controlled these secondary schools, they were often referred to as 'County Schools'. Pupils entered them at 11 and most stayed until the first public examination at 16, the General School Examination; a small number stayed till 18 for the Higher School Examination. There was no other generally available kind of State secondary school apart from these grammar schools, but the more energetic local authorities increasingly set up separate post-primary schools, called variously 'central', 'senior' or 'modern' schools, for selected children over 11. The London County Council had pioneered their central schools before 1914; they enjoyed a high reputation. The Hadow Report of 1926 on the Education of the Adolescent had recommended that this system be made universal; but, by 1939, 46 per cent of all children in the State system were still being educated in the traditional, all-age-range elementary school.

Thus the universal break at 11, with differing forms of secondary education for children over that age, established by the Butler Act of 1944, was the implementation of a reform which, though its necessity had been realized for a generation, had been held back by the Depression and by the distaste of the times for the expenditure of public money for the public good. Likewise, more informal teaching methods, the belief that education was not solely concerned with intellectual attainment and that intellectual attainment itself was not to be measured solely in terms of the quantity of facts memorized—all these, like intelligence testing and the idea that drama and movement and opportunities for free expression were also part of education, were already current in the mid twenties, but adopted only piecemeal. The most publicized pacemaker in educational change was A. S. Neill, whose private school at Summerhill (chiefly for the problem children of the rich) dispensed with discipline in the conventional sense, left pupils to express themselves as they wished and treated them as having equal rights with adults. Bertrand Russell and his wife, Dora, also ran a school

London elementary schoolchildren about 1925. The boots and jersey were common wear

of a not dissimilar nature in the twenties. The so-called 'Dalton Plan', which left children free to teach themselves through independent work on assignments merely supervised by their teachers, was also widely advocated though rarely practised. The most effective pioneers of change, however, were probably those in the training colleges who trained the infants' school-teachers of the time. Infants' schools grew noticeably more relaxed in the thirties, partly because they were inevitably child-centred and less dominated by academic tradition. But all sections of the State system suffered from cramped buildings and lack of finance, while the State grammar schools remained convinced that innovations which departed from the public school traditions they sought to emulate would mean a 'lowering of standards'.

Generalizations about life in the elementary schools of the period are dangerous, since schools were as varied as the variable quality of their staffs and their social environment. The view that they were grimly regimented, relied heavily on corporal punishment and made children's lives a misery is exaggerated. Small rural schools and the smaller Church schools anywhere could be extremely amiable. And even if the under-sevens of the time sat in rows learning the alphabet by chanting 'A says ER, B says BER, C says KER', they did not regard the process with disapproval. The choric *sprachgesang* by which multiplication tables were fixed for ever in the mind had its own interior dynamic. It rose to a climax at 'TEN-sevens-are-SEVENTY', followed by a coda in which the joyful simplicity of 'Eleven-sevens-are-seventy-seven' was contrasted with the joyful triumph over the intellectually abstruse of 'TWELVE-sevens-are-Eighty-FOUR!' Neither the hideousness of the buildings nor the size of the classes (anything from 50 to 60) seemed to distress children; their homes were probably even more hideous and relatively no less crowded. Large schools in difficult urban areas could be formidable enough, with a proportion of their staffs eager to secure peace and quiet for themselves by a frequent use of the cane, but even the more savage elementary schools applied corporal punishment in a fairly informal manner, and ritualized beatings were not normal. Indeed, it is possible to suggest that

The 'top class' (of forty-five boys) in a North Kensington, London, elementary school, 1923. They came from a relatively prosperous area on the outskirts of Notting Hill

one great difference between the ethos of an elementary school and that of the independent preparatory or public school was that whereas the latter taught boys not to be cowards, elementary schools taught them not to be bullies.

In general, the elementary schools were well ordered rather than seriously repressive; and since they imposed fewer intellectual demands on their pupils and insisted less exactingly on conformity to rigid patterns of behaviour, they might have fewer disciplinary problems than secondary schools, particularly as they did not retain their pupils after they were 14. What impressed many elementary school-teachers about their pupils was the inadequacy of their clothing, their diet and their personal hygiene, rather than their unruliness. The most frequent interruption of elementary school routine was the visit of the school nurse who, with the aid of a steel comb repeatedly immersed in carbolic, searched the children's heads for nits. To be infected by other children's headlice was one of the major hazards of elementary school life. And when the population of the urban elementary schools was evacuated to the residential rural counties in 1939 it was the manifestly low standard of the

102

home life they were used to that provoked shocked complaint, not their violence or delinquency. Public displays of juvenile disorderliness were characteristic only of university students.

There was a great deal of marching about and lining up and an elaborate saluting of the Union Jack on Empire Day (24 May) and, in maintained no less than Church schools, much learning of *Hymns, Ancient and Modern*. There was much grammar, dictation and composition, much learning of poetry by heart, almost all of it from the literary warhorses of the nineteenth century, as was the substance of the reading lessons, and endless arithmetic, though neither algebra nor geometry. There was drawing, chiefly of kettles and draped sheets, but often no painting. The drill lesson occupied the place later given over to 'physical education'. It took place in hall or playground and without such refinements as changing out of ordinary clothing; the time was spent chiefly in obeying the commands, arms stretch, knees bend, breathe in, breathe out. Music meant singing lessons (with anything up to 100 children at a time) involving, of course, hymns, 'God Bless the Prince of Wales', ''Twas in Trafalgar Bay' and the singing teachers' favourite, 'Blow Away The Morning Dew'. The final act of the infants' school day could well be the singing of 'Now The Day Is Over, Night Is Drawing Nigh', shortly after three o'clock in the afternoon.

Girls' County School orchestra, 1923. The teachers have not bobbed their hair

The quality of the men and women who entered the elementary schools between the wars was high, if only because there was only limited scope for ex-secondary school sixth-formers in industry and commerce (particularly for girls) and because few of them could go to a university. Elementary school-teaching was still as much a man's job as a woman's since the sexes were segregated once children ceased, at the age of seven, to be Mixed Infants and 'went up into the Big Boys' or the 'Big Girls'. There was a marked contrast between the younger teachers and those who had done most of their service before 1914. These older men and women tended to be hard, grumpy characters, aggressively determined to have no nonsense. The attention they secured tended to expose their deficiencies both as teachers and as persons.

To get to a grammar (i.e. secondary) school it was necessary to pass a competitive examination at 10 plus. The examination for prospective fee-payers was not very searching, unless it was an exceptional school. Those who sought a free place had a harder examination. For those who wanted a junior county scholarship which carried a local education authority grant, the test was still harder; and as it was purely an attainment test in English, arithmetic and general knowledge, the curriculum of the junior school tended to concentrate overmuch on getting as many of the brightest children as possible 'through the scholarship'. In the main, it was the scholarship boy and girl who set the pace in the secondary schools and greatly improved the quality of their academic work. Fee-paying pupils often did not complete the full course. The secondary schools' principal object soon became that of getting their pupils to pass the General School Examination at 16 and if possible to secure matriculation exemption as a result. 'Passing Matric' necessitated passing (at around 50 per cent) in mathematics, English language and literature (counted together as one subject), Latin or science, a modern foreign language and two other subjects, all at one and the same sitting; failure in any one subject meant retaking the whole examination. A really good secondary school was one in which to 'get General Schools' but not Matric was to have 'failed'.

Secondary schools rapidly developed sixth forms after 1919. These were encouraged by local authority grants and the annual award by the Board of Education of 200 State Scholarships to enable sixth-form pupils to go to university. There were also teacher-training scholarships. The London County Council, an extremely forward-looking authority, awarded free tuition and scholarships worth up to £39 a year to enable pupils to stay on after the General School Examination. Local authorities also gave grants to help sixth-formers to go to university, but the student had to pay his fees out of such grants and the amount varied widely from county to county. In many areas these awards were made only to winners of open university scholarships. The winner of an open Oxbridge award would receive over £170 if he lived in London but only £90 if he lived in Kent. Some authorities gave grants only to recipients who certified they were too poor to pay their own fees, but paid out cheques only after receiving proof that students' fees had in fact been paid.

Almost the only pupils in full-time education whose expenses were covered by grants were the fortunate 200 who annually won State Scholarships. It was thus not merely the difficulty of getting a place or a grant that kept people out of university; it was also the fact that only parents with settled jobs and earnings well above the national average who could afford to supplement the inadequate grants paid to their children by the authorities. Lower down the scale, the junior county

Visually aided geography lesson in the yard of a village school in Yorkshire, 1930

The first new secondary school built in London after the 1914–18 war. Opened in 1926 at a cost of £56,000, it was characteristic of school building between the wars

scholarship, though entitling the child to attend secondary school till 16, like the intermediate scholarship which might enable him to go on to 18, neither covered the inevitable extra expenses involved nor compensated parents for the loss of the child's earnings. That 70 per cent of all children began earning at 14 and over 90 per cent of them at 15 is indicative not merely of lack of educational opportunity but of the hard economic fact that working-class and lower middle-class earnings were unequal to the cost of maintaining an adolescent who, by staying at school, added to the expenses of a household while contributing nothing to its income. Nor could this problem be eased by week-end or holiday jobs; with between

1·5 and 2 million regularly unemployed such jobs were not available. Doing a newspaper round was the only work of this kind that was available. Accordingly, in the industrial areas, many parents did not let their children take up secondary-school places even if they won scholarships; and most secondary pupils left at 16 since this was the normal age of entry, for example, into law, accountancy, banking and insurance. Employees attached little value to the Higher School Certificate, and often had not heard of it. The sixth form was, therefore, reserved for a tiny minority who would enter teaching, the civil service, nursing and university courses. Many of these would moreover find themselves a drug on the market from 1931 onwards. The unemployed or underemployed ex-secondary-school graduate was a common phenomenon of the thirties. There would normally be 200 applicants at least for any good teaching post; and J. B. Priestley records in his *English Journey* meeting a graduate engineer from Oxford who at the age of 30 was working for Daimler's in 1933 for as little as £4 a week, which was no more than the national

LCC Elementary School String Orchestra, 1935

Modern classroom, 1936. Evidence in the children's appearance of the rising standards of living in more prosperous areas. School milk was issued during the thirties at a cost of a halfpenny for two-thirds of a pint

average wage of the time. In these circumstances, it is not surprising that of those in full-time education in 1934, only 1 per cent were in universities, technical or teacher-training colleges and that only 6 per cent of secondary pupils reached university. Of elementary-school pupils, only 4 in 1,000 went to university and only 1 in 1,000 to Oxford or Cambridge.

Although the statistics show that they catered for a small, if growing, section of the population, the grammar schools flourished between the wars. They provided the only bridge, narrow though it was, by which the gulf between the classes might be crossed. They could rescue the academic child from the financially and culturally deprived life of the industrial working class; or propel the child of the small shopkeeper or minor civil servant up into realms hitherto the preserve of the alumni of the public schools. It was their consciousness of this mission that gave the grammar schools their purposiveness, their prestige, their arrogant sense of being more important than the elementary schools and more socially dynamic than the public schools; and it was this, too, that seemed to justify the superiority of their salary scale to that enjoyed by elementary-school teachers. And since they provided a third of all university students by the thirties, they contributed much to the raising of university academic standards, particularly at Oxford and Cambridge. The basic condition of entry to these universities for fee-payers (or gentlemen commoners) was the ability to pass the Previous Examination, which was well below the standard of the Matric that the secondary pupil took; and many gentlemen commoners contented themselves with an Ordinary degree, the attainment of which required a minimum of intellectual effort. The contrast between such idle, if personable, young men from independent schools and the large number of much abler and not much less personable young men from the secondary schools who did not go to university was one of the more deplorable features of the time.

Less serious perhaps was the superior attitude of Oxbridge to the provincial universities, which had not yet acquired the irrationally derogatory label 'Redbrick'. The provincial universities had never aspired to imitate the Oxbridge tradition of being playgrounds for the sons of the rich, and their examinations were always alleged to be much harder than Oxbridge degree examinations. Oxbridge responded by referring to them as 'little better than glorified night schools' and by claiming that they catered only for 'students', whereas Oxbridge had 'undergraduates', who were altogether more rounded personalities. In practical terms this sometimes meant little more than that they played more games, consumed more alcohol and took a livelier interest in barmaids, waitresses and shopgirls.

The public schools suffered in those years from a good deal of adverse publicity, much of it emanating from their own former pupils. Alec Waugh's novel *The Loom of Youth* was only the first of a number of books to depict the public schools in an unflattering light; and the predominantly left-wing intellectuals of the thirties regularly asserted of their old schools that they were brutalizing, that they encouraged excessive athleticism, a dubiously complacent form of Christianity, an unthinking patriotism and were narrowly class-conscious. The obverse of this was to be found in the many somewhat gushing accounts

Eton boys arriving at Lord's for the Eton v Harrow cricket match, 1934

of what were called 'romantic friendships' among public schoolboys. The strongest evidence of the restrictiveness and conformism of the public schools was the almost unanimous testimony of their products to the exhilarating sense of personal and intellectual liberation they experienced on arriving at Oxford or Cambridge. The first impressions of Oxbridge of a scholarship boy from a State day-school might be of finding himself immured in a world of small rituals and taboos, nastily furnished rooms, inferior plumbing and, perhaps for the whole of his first term, personal loneliness.

Both at secondary school and at university, the scholarship boy of this period was a social pioneer, the precursor of the much later invasion of the whole field of higher education by the recipients of State subsidies. He displayed some of the rather unlikeable characteristics of E. M. Forster's Leonard Bast or of Aldous Huxley's Frank Illidge, though virtually never those of a Lucky Jim, since he was not a boozy barbarian. He tended to be priggish and to look down on the working classes without acquiring the easy self-confidence of the upper classes. The impression he might sometimes create is suggested by the remark of a prominent figure in the City of London who wrote in 1934, 'I have come across several cases of secondary pupils who have passed all sorts of examinations but who are unable to obtain employment owing to defects of personality.' If such a scholarship boy succeeded in life he might be careful not to reveal that he had never been to a public school; and if he did not succeed he might resent the little reward his years of arduous academic struggle had earned him and believe that it was his inferior social origin that was the true cause of this. This resentment afflicted the boy whose parents had not been able to keep him at school into the sixth form, and the sixth-former who had not managed to get to university, no less than the graduate with a poor job or no job. Accordingly, the effect of the grammar school in dissolving class differences between the wars can be over-estimated. In one sense, the grammar school sharpened them, by making an intelligent, but often under-utilized and sometimes unemployed minority more conscious than they might have been of the contrast between the deprivations endured by the many and the privileges enjoyed by the few.

No survey of education between the wars is complete without reference to the many 'private schools' which flourished, mainly in the southern part of the country, providing a fee-paying alternative to the State elementary and sometimes the State grammar schools. The many day-schools of this type were some-times carried on in quite small private houses by a husband and wife and sought to compensate for their manifold shortcomings by the garishness of their school uniform and their emphasis on correct social behaviour. Their fees were perforce low and so, therefore, were the salaries they paid any assistant teachers they employed. These assistants were without pension rights and had virtually no security of tenure. Such schools existed solely because of the determination of a certain number of parents to prevent their offspring being contaminated either by the diseases or the bad language of 'common' children. Many small prepara-tory and 12-plus boarding-schools had similar characteristics, often providing the lowest of academic standards, the strangest headmasters and head-mistresses and the most ineffective and eccen-tric of teachers. Since such institutions were virtually beyond the reach of supervisory legislation or statistical assessment, it can only be recorded that they ranged from a level not much above that of

Primary group in a new school in 1937, a further indication of the progress made in some parts of the country

Dotheboys Hall to the awe-inspiring but ultimately unverifiable status of 'almost a public school'.

Further Reading

S. J. Curtis, *Education in England since 1900*, 1952. Apart from works mentioned in the text, the effects of public-school life may be studied in Cyril Connolly, *Enemies of Promise*, 1938, and Lord Lytton, *Anthony, A Record of Youth*. Since Orwell was an Old Etonian as well as a Socialist, the several references in *The Road to Wigan Pier* to 'pansy poets' and the lofty assertion that no decent person wanted to have anything to do with vegetarians are oddly revealing. I am unaware of any autobiography or novel which provides a generally valid picture of the elementary schools. Accounts of school and university life by dons, headmasters, 'educationists' and well-known literary personalities should be read with the utmost caution.

VII

Words, Words, Words

By 1930 compulsory education of a sort had been universal for about half a century, the cinema was barely 30 years old, the wireless comparatively new and television a matter for the future. For information and entertainment a higher proportion of the population relied mainly on the printed word than in the past or the future. Although by 1939 only 67 per cent of adults bought a daily paper, the total circulation of the national dailies had risen from under 4·5 million in 1910 to 10·5 million; and the total of annual borrowings from public libraries rose from 85·6 million in 1924 to 207·9 million in 1939. And while it is possible to hazard the guess that compulsory education tended to make the lower classes more orderly and less alienated from society than in the past, it is also likely that the informal educators, persuaders and entertainers who used the medium of print were more effective moulders of the popular mind than were the school-teachers.

The first use to which a child might put his nascent reading powers would be to take in the pages of the *Rainbow* comic, with its front page devoted to Tiger Tim and the Bruin Boys, a merry collection of miscellaneous animals dressed in school uniforms and but imperfectly controlled by Mrs Bruin, who combined the qualities of a Mummy Bear with those of the mob-capped mistress of an early dame school. The colour was a cheap red and the draughtsmanship pre-Disney with no undertones of violence. The text was pre-Enid Blyton and without pretensions to the goody-goody. From there, a child might progress to the black-and-white grossness of *Film Fun*, cashing in on the popularity of the early screen comics, and then to the *Gem* and *Magnet*

Billy Bunter, the Owl of Greyfriars, proves a bully as well as a fat coward. But Bob and Harry will soon put things to rights.
(The Magnet, *September 1920*)

for which, for so many years, Frank Richards wrote stories of Tom Merry & Co. of St Jim's and Harry Wharton & Co. of Greyfriars. Frank Richards' inexhaustible inventiveness made these stories of the scrapes of the strongly characterized members of the Shell and the Remove in these two imaginary boarding-schools the most compulsive reading. The writer's supreme creation was Billy Bunter, a fat, cowardly, doughnut-guzzling, money-cadging boy who may properly rank as the Falstaff of juvenile fiction.

Adventure was catered for in the twenties by *Chums* and the *Boy's Own Paper*, the latter long retaining among boys' magazines the status enjoyed by *The Times* among the dailies. It was recommended by clergymen and head masters as being 'healthy'. In the thirties, ordinary boys preferred the more plebeian *Hotspur* and *Wizard*. 'Sexton Blake' stories were widely read also and, as they were published, Richmal Crompton's 'Just William' stories, about an ink-stained, tousle-haired 11-year-old boy for ever innocently creating chaos in the middle-class suburbia to which an inconsiderate fate had condemned him. He bore little resemblance to any living child of the period. Among more solid writers, a ballot taken at the Schoolboys' Exhibition in 1926 appeared to show that the favourite authors at that date were R. M. Ballantyne, G. A. Henty, Conan Doyle, Rider Haggard, Jules Verne, Captain Marryat, Kipling, Dickens, Westerman, Kingsley, Talbot Baines Reed, Fenimore Cooper and Scott, in that order. Ballantyne's most attractive book was *Coral Island*. Conan Doyle was probably in on account of Sherlock Holmes, Kipling because of *Kim* and the *Just So Stories* and Kingsley because of *Westward Ho!*, a book which fixed irremovably on thousands of impressionable minds its own particular image of Elizabethan sea-dogs and of Spanish Catholicism. The inclusion of Dickens and Scott was a gesture of respect to the grown-ups and both Marryat and Jules Verne were coming to be thought 'heavy'. So were Henty and Fenimore Cooper, who belonged to the already fading traditions of the hey-day of popular Imperialist sentiment. Rider Haggard's *King Solomon's Mines* proved very durable, however.

Talbot Baines Reed qualified as a popular writer of school stories, a widely read genre to which P. G. Wodehouse also contributed. The popularity of stories about prep schools and public schools among children who attended State schools was phenomenal and not confined to boys. Not only was *Schoolgirl's Own* devoted to tales about girls' boarding-schools; some of the most deliciously 'period' writing of the time is to be found in the school stories of the wildly successful Angela Brazil.

For self-improvement, the young of the period could turn to the greatest children's journalist of all time, Arthur Mee. He was responsible for *The Children's Encyclopaedia*, founded *The Children's Newspaper* in 1919 and then the illustrated monthly, *My Magazine*. The first was in the home of almost every child with parents thoughtful enough (and not too poor) to buy it. *The Children's Newspaper* presented the weekly news, domestic and foreign, lucidly but reflectively and without sensationalism. It ran little campaigns, such as commending the LCC for not naming public houses on the destination blinds of its trams and reproving the London General Omnibus Company for continuing to do so on the destination boards of its buses. A typical issue of *My Magazine* might contain an article on Hugh Myddleton and the New River or on Paracelsus and alchemy, a set of reproductions headed 'Why All France Loves Watteau', an article about thyroid extract, adrenal glands, hormones and 'vitamines' (in the very early twenties) or an illustrated warning captioned 'What London Will Look Like if the War Men are Allowed to Force Another War'. Pictures of bombed buildings were combined with such prophecies, 20 years before the event, as 'in the next war aerial torpedoes will knock out whole lines of motor lorries supplying the troops'. Arthur Mee was

The front page of The Children's Newspaper, *5th April 1919*, reporting the newest developments in 'the wireless telephone' and forecasting aeroplane speeds of 800 mph. The layout and writing are a careful adaptation of the styles of a contemporary adult newspaper

grave but not pompous, benevolent but not sentimental. No writer for the young so successfully avoided being either patronizing or archly jolly.

Middle-class children were brought up on Beatrix Potter, *The Wind in the Willows*, *Peter Pan* and *Alice*. Beatrix Potter's illustrations and Kenneth Grahame's prose probably provided urban children with their most abiding notions about the recently vanished rural past; but no one ever knew quite what children made of *Alice* or whether a working-class child could have made anything of *Peter Pan* at all.

The adult educators of the twenties were still Shaw and Wells. *Avant-garde* writers like T. S. Eliot, Joyce, Virginia Woolf and even Lytton Strachey, D. H. Lawrence and Aldous Huxley influenced the future rather than their immediate contemporaries, save for the most sophisticated among them. Shaw had little to say that was new and not much that was sensible in the twenties, but Wells, always less of a gadfly than Shaw, persisted in his efforts to fill the gaps left in the minds of the earnest-minded young by their teachers. He outlined history and also science, and produced *The Wealth, Work and Happiness of Mankind, The World of William Clissold, The Open Conspiracy* and *The Shape of Things To Come*, all condemned by academics as superficial and by the literary as a tedious misuse of Wells's talent, but all with something valid to say about the human condition. His *Outline History of the World*, though justly criticized as the work of one who had written more history than he had read, was a challenge to the parochially national, or at best West European, preoccupations of academic historians that they have since found it impossible to ignore. J. B. Priestley, who tried to entertain as well as edify, was even less popular with the critics. A best-selling success, *The Good Companions*, was followed by *Angel Pavement* which, though less popular, is a useful portrayal of the moods of the early thirties; and his *English Journey*, published in 1933, offers incomparably the most reliable survey of what England was really like at that time.

The great advance in the thirties was the birth of the paperback. Allen Lane published the first Penguins in 1935, at 6*d.* each, thus making reprints of fairly recent books widely available for the first time. The most successful predecessors to Penguins were the 6*d.* hardback Readers' Library series, sold by Woolworth's, which offered only 'classics' on which copyright had expired, and had small print and bad paper. The first two Penguins were *Ariel*, a study of Shelley by André Maurois, and Ernest Hemingway's *A Farewell To Arms*. Pelicans appeared soon afterwards, with a rather more deliberately educational character, early titles including *Practical Economics* by G. D. H. Cole, *Essays in Popular Science* by Julian Huxley and *The Mysterious Universe* by Sir James Jeans, a book

The first sixpenny Penguin, 1935, and an early Pelican

which almost made physics comprehensible to laymen. A Penguin Shakespeare had begun to appear by 1937. Also significant were the Penguin Specials appearing from the end of 1937, dealing with the contemporary European situation. The first of these, Edgar Mowrer's *Germany Puts The Clock Back*, sold out in a week and was reprinted four times in four months.

Penguins revolutionized publishing not only by what they were but by the imitators they inspired. The triumph of the paperback was both a response to and an encouragement of the rising educational standards of the time and proved that cinema and radio and all the other new rival forms of leisure activity had not, after all, destroyed the reading habit. Indeed, people in the thirties were such inveterate readers that 'Twopenny Libraries' appeared in many towns. These were shops from which anybody could borrow any book in stock for twopence with a minimum of formality. Sub-post offices ran lending libraries; and enterprising persons even made money on the side by taking books round the housing estates on the backs of bicycles to lend to young wives housebound by the baby. The formula was simple: the circulating librarian asked his customer, 'Would you like a Romance or a Western?' and selected an appropriate volume.

A spate of anti-war books dominated the scene in the early thirties: a translation of the German *All Quiet on the Western Front*, Richard Aldington's *Death of a Hero*, Vera Brittain's *Testament of Youth* and Beverley Nichols's *Cry Havoc!* were among the most popular. The late thirties produced the phenomenon of the Left Book Club, founded by the publisher, Victor Gollancz. This, the first of the book clubs, had 60,000 members, who received monthly a book chosen for them by Gollancz and two Marxist sympathizers, John Strachey and Harold Laski. The choices were designed to alert members to the menace of Fascism and the evils of unplanned capitalism. Members were encouraged to form Left Book Club groups to study the monthly choices and to promote the formation of a Popular Front of all who believed that Fascism should be 'resisted'. The Club published Orwell's *The Road to Wigan Pier* and first brought Arthur

Koestler to the notice of the reading public. Other offerings varied from textbooks of Marxism to accounts of life in areas of unemployment, especially Ellen Wilkinson's account of Jarrow, *The Town That Was Murdered*. None of the Club's aims—to 'resist' Fascism, to save Republican Spain from Franco, to overthrow Chamberlain and revitalize the Labour Party—was achieved, but its publications shaped the thinking of many of those who were to vote Labour into power in 1945, and the existence of the Club was one of the many signs of a growing dissatisfaction with the character of English society and politics during the late thirties.

The literature of entertainment was characterized by the growing vogue for the detective story. For many it replaced the manly adventure story produced earlier by Conan Doyle, John Buchan (*The Thirty-nine Steps*) and Sapper, who wrote *Bulldog Drummond* and had a 1920-ish scorn for Jews and Bolshies. For others it took the place of the pot-boiling thrillers produced in quantity in the twenties by Edgar Wallace, who, in 1928, had dramatizations of three of his stories running simultaneously in the West End. The detective story almost always had an upper middle-class setting and deducing from the author's clues the identity of the murderer had, as has been observed, something of the fascination exercised by crossword puzzles, which began as a craze in the twenties and became a national institution in the thirties. The most prolific detective-story writer was already Agatha Christie; but in the thirties, Dorothy L. Sayers wrote successful stories, including *The Nine Tailors* and *Gaudy Night*, featuring an elegant, witty and exquisitely cultured detective called Lord Peter Wimsey. He was like a sophisticated adman's updating of the Baroness Orczy's Sir Percy Blakeney, whose admirers were still numerous.

P. G. Wodehouse, noted in the early twenties mainly as a writer of school stories, of 'light' novels and of the 'books' of various musicals, gradually developed into a national cult, chiefly as the creator of Jeeves and Bertie Wooster. When first written, his work was representative of a popular fashion for frivolous stories about upper class young men who were short of cash and had trouble with grumpy elders and unresponsive

VOGUE

APRÈS LA TEMPÊTE.

Cover page of Vogue, *1919. Enigmatic but obviously elated young person in apparently elegant surroundings*

or independent-minded young women; and the failure of such young men's education to equip them for work (or even for the correct quotation of the lines of Shakespeare) was a not unfamiliar phenomenon.

The improving social and economic status of women led to a boom in women's magazines. *Vogue* had been founded in 1916 and *Harper's Bazaar* began in 1929, for the sophisticated daughters of mothers who had been satisfied with the more discreet pages of *The Lady*, founded in 1885, and *The Queen*, which dated back to 1861. There came into existence a group of relatively expensive and lavish monthlies catering for the growing taste for 'modernity' in the home. *Homes and Gardens* came in 1919, *Woman and Home* in 1926 and *Woman's Journal* in 1927. For the working-class woman and her growing-up daughter a number of new weeklies kept up the old tradition of romantic fiction with a 'strong' emotional line: *True Story* was founded in 1922, *Red Star Weekly* in 1929 and *True Romances* and *Family Star* in 1934. The publications with the broadest appeal were the weeklies containing short stories and serials, together with features made up of knitting patterns, recipes, tips about dress, accessories and makeup, a short quasi-religious article (allegedly, very often, by a pipe-smoking, slightly greying man of comforting appearance looking out over a country stile) or a piece about the nicer emotions by such writers as Godfrey Winn or Beverley Nichols, and an advice column about boyfriends, office romances and what to wear for a christening.

To begin with, *Home Notes* and *Family Journal* met this demand; but the enduring *Woman's Weekly*, begun in 1911, quietly paved the way for the more colourful *Woman's Own* (1932) and *Woman* (1937). Magazines of this latter sort provided almost the only available advice that many young women and young mothers could get about clothes, diet, relations with the other sex, bringing up children, and general home management. The advice offered was safe and sensible, impeccably conventional in morality and devoid of intellectual content. The complex of activities associated with falling in (or out of) love, having a husband, a home and a family was treated wholly in isolation from everything else and as the absolute sum of female existence. From first page to last, sex was also taboo. In consequence these magazines were much criticized by thoughtful people; but most younger women found

Cover page, No. 1 of Woman, *June 1937. The glowingly healthy young woman wears a sun hat to denote unaffected simplicity and a low dress to suggest the right blend of the erotic with the maternal*

Woman *announces its comprehensive advice service. 'Write to us about your woes, whatever they are'*

Let us help you

BEAUTY

Henrietta Trimble has been associated with the leading women pioneers in beauty culture and has studied—and still studies—both with chemists and doctors, including a famous dermatologist. Has given beauty culture develop from a luxury to a necessity within the means of every ordinary woman.

FASHION

Alison Settle, England's first Fashion Advisor and consultant. Has a flair for picking out the style points each season and helping every woman to look her best—at a reasonable cost ! Appointed a member of the Council of Art and Industry by the Board of Trade.

ART OF LIVING

Jacqueline Howard has learnt the art of turning houses into homes in all sorts of circumstances—in large houses in the country and small ones in town, seaside cottages and tiny London flats. Has lived in Italy, Mexico and Spain, Holland, Switzerland and France.

Inquiries

Now you know the gifted experts who are at your service, we hope that you will feel even more friendly—and don't forget that the essence of friendship is helpfulness !

Simply address your queries to the expert in question, at WOMAN, Martlett House, Martlett Court, 31, Bow Street, Strand, London, W.C.2. Enclose a stamped addressed envelope.

We don't mind if we're flooded out with letters, and you'll certainly still see us smiling when you get us out from underneath the biggest postal delivery on record !

All we ask is to be given the opportunity of helping each of our readers in her own individual problem.

FURNISHING

Kathleen A. Pearcey believes simplicity and fitness of purpose are essential either in a single piece of furniture or in a whole room. Collects big ideas—found in many countries—and adapts them successfully to small homes. Expert with decoration, but just as interested in kitchens and linen cupboards.

HOUSEKEEPING

Susan Strong feels that a year of practical experience is worth ten of theory. Is competent to judge. Two years training in cookery and household management. Two years Superintendent of a woman's club. Working housekeeper on a farm, where she baked bread, made butter and looked after six children !

Next week

"HERE comes the bride. . . ." Yes, and WOMAN has dressed her—at least, suggested the design for her frock ; has shown her the way to radiant beauty and given her anxious mother inspiration on the entertainment question so that she can sit in her pew minus a furrowed brow !

Our next issue turns the spotlight on the June bride. We tell her just how she can be attired in the style of her millionaire-sisters-under-the-skin ; how her beauty may hit the top standard of the most affluent beauty salons, and how she may bear herself with such dignity as may even

COOKERY

Moira Meighn : A famous French chef offered her lessons in the kitchen of an hotel that has made restaurant history. Has cooked under all conditions. Often an emergency cook for doctor's patients in country cottages. Tests all her recipes. Gave the first television demonstration of cookery.

CHILD CARE

Experts in Council ! This feature will be planned by the wife of a doctor—herself the mother of four children. Nursery topics will be handled by Sister Just, whose work as health visitor, founder of baby clubs, lecturer and welfare-centre consultant has well fitted her for the job !

become a princess of the royal purple.

And apart from all this practical advice —we offer words of wisdom through ANDRE MAUROIS, the great philosopher, who takes for his address " Rules for a Happy Marriage."

FICTION—there was a girl involved in an accident, who found the perfect host— another determined female who earned her right to stardom (celluloid), a young couple who found their romance curiously linked with processions—and the final instalment of " Laughter Makes Life."

There will be help galore from our Council of Seven and entertaining articles into the bargain.

Woman

out on Thursday, June 17

one or other of them indispensable and in the main they had a civilizing influence which was much underrated by their critics.

Newspapers were now big business, run for profit and controlled by wealthy Press lords who, though often good journalists, were also ruthless bosses. Since the masses could not afford to pay the real cost of newspapers produced by the million, newspapers increasingly depended on advertisement revenue; and they could not attract advertising unless they had a mass audience. Newspaper production, therefore, though highly profitable, was intensely competitive, and the period saw a rapid decline in the number of independent provincial dailies and a fall even in the number of national dailies. There was a decline in their political content, and a tendency to sensationalize and trivialize. Increasingly, newspapers had to entertain their readers. They were also considered at the time to be unduly influenced not only by the advertisers on whom they depended but also by the excessive political ambitions of their wealthy owners. In practice, advertisers were interested solely in the size or quality of a newspaper's circulation, while the Press lords of the time were conspicuous political failures.

Those who rejected the newer mass Press read *The Times*, which contrived despite many financial vicissitudes to retain its old air of authority. It was the last of the dailies to begin printing pictures. When it did so, its older readers were grieved. Control of its shares was vested in an imposing group of trustees yet, paradoxically, *The Times* was perhaps the one paper whose policy was most seriously affected by the influence of an individual: its Editor, Geoffrey Dawson, went to unusual

Cartoon by Poy, Evening News, *18 December 1926. Rich young Oswald Mosley, having left the Tories, contests Smethwick for Labour (and wins). Three stereotypes of the time (working class appearance, the dotty Socialist theorist, the bewhiskered Bolshevik) and use of the Communist bogey*

GOING OVER?

FLAPPER: " Which one shall I throw it at, Fido ? " *April 22nd, 1927.*

Cartoon by Strube, Daily Express, *22 April 1927. 'I want To Be Happy' was a hit song from* No, No, Nanette

lengths to make *The Times* an obstinate partisan of Chamberlain's policy of appeasing Hitler. More rigorously old-fashioned Tories chose the *Morning Post*; but with a circulation of under 200,000 it was absorbed into the *Daily Telegraph* in 1937. The *Daily Telegraph*, selling 640,000 copies by 1939, was the particular choice of businessmen, its most valuable selling asset being its situations vacant columns, daily scanned by black-coated workers in search of employment. Its tone was acidly Conservative (but hostile to Hitler) and its news service workmanlike and comprehensive.

Liberal, 'progressive' readers were decreasingly catered for. By 1930 their only national daily was the *News Chronicle*, formed by the merger in 1930 of the *Daily News* and the *Daily Chronicle*. Each had been selling nearly a million copies daily, but by 1930 this was not large enough to attract adequate advertising revenue. Controlled by the Cadbury family and with the format of a popular daily, the *News Chronicle* was a committed anti-Conservative, anti-Fascist paper. In consequence it sold fewer copies than the other popular dailies. Its partner, the London evening *Star*, always sold well, punters greatly esteeming its racing tips. The *Manchester Guardian* was Liberalism's other mouthpiece; one of the few provincial dailies that still flourished, its reputation was greater than its circulation owing to its tradition of probity and irreproachable highmindedness.

The pacemaker of journalism for the masses had been the *Daily Mail*, founded in 1896 and supported by the *Evening News* and *Sunday Dispatch*. Owned by Alfred Harmsworth, Lord Northcliffe, and after his death in 1922 by his brother, Lord Rothermere, the *Dail Mail* already carried in the twenties the proud rhyme 'Daily Mail, One Million Sale'. In the 1930s it

Front page of Daily Mail, *1 June 1926, then the most expensive advertising sp*

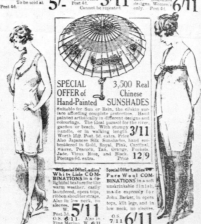
ailies. Techniques are primitive, and as many words as possible are crowded in

was surpassed by the *Daily Express*, controlled, like the *Evening Standard* and *Sunday Express*, by Max Aitken, Lord Beaverbrook, and also by the *Daily Herald*. The *Daily Herald*, at first a struggling supporter of the Labour Party, became in 1929 the joint financial responsibility of the Trade Union Congress and Odhams Press. It immediately entered the lists for the mass market and provoked a circulation war. The rivals tried to outdo one another in attracting readers with the bait of free insurance and free gifts. Door-to-door canvassers lured house-holders into buying one of these papers for a number of weeks in order to qualify for bound volumes of Dickens, the memoirs of Lloyd George, the prefaces of Bernard Shaw, encyclopaedias and the like. It is a comment on the employment situation of the time that there was no difficulty in finding 50,000 men to do this canvassing. The outcome of a most costly struggle was victory for the *Daily Express*. It was selling 2,486,000 copies in 1939. The *Daily Herald* sold 2 million, the *Daily Mail* 1,510,000 and the *News Chronicle* 1,317,000.

The *Daily Express* triumphed because it was best attuned to the mood of the thirties. The *Daily Mail* had flourished in the more strident political atmosphere of the first 30 years of the century, raging furiously against Socialism, Bolshevism and the League of Nations which was supported, so the *Daily Mail* would say, 'by lovers of every country but their own'. For the *Daily Express*, brightness was all. It took nothing seriously (unless it was unimportant), even confidently assuring its readers in 1939, 'There will be no war this year—or next.' It did not ignore the news: its reporters were extremely able, its eye for a scoop and for the crispest, liveliest, presentation of it unrivalled; but it contrived to trivialize home affairs and to treat the repeated international crises of the thirties as no real concern of its readers save as a reminder of how much better everything was in England. It rarely supported any cause, except for Empire Free Trade, which was a fantasy of Beaverbrook's own and which his readers ignored as blithely as they did the menace of Hitler. Though it was never for 'top people' the *Daily Express* managed to appeal to most social classes; and its manner and its technical efficiency prevented it ever meriting Lord Salisbury's gibe against the early *Daily Mail*—that it was written 'for office boys by office boys'.

The *Daily Express*, no doubt because of the Canadian Presbyterian upbringing of its proprietor, disliked Europe and anything cultural and also made almost no use of sex; and this helped to sell it in the thirties. By that time, those in search of sensational sex in their newspaper were still relying heavily on the best-selling paper of all, Lord Riddell's *News of the World*, which sold nearly 4 million copies every Sunday in 1939. It was regarded as preferred reading by the British working man while enjoying his 'lie-in' on Sunday morning. Its pages were rich in news items with such headings as 'Young Girl's Ordeal' or 'Elderly Business Man on Grave Charge'.

The return of excitement to the daily Press came with a change of policy in the *Daily Mirror* towards the end of the thirties. Like the *Daily Sketch*, it was a small-format 'picture paper' originally intended to attract women, who were, of course, too feather-headed to be able to read a lot of print. The circulation figures of the two papers were closely similar until the *Daily Mirror* took to using the biggest and blackest headlines ever seen in England and to bedecking its pages with pictures of girls. The most scantily clad of the *Daily Mirror*'s young women was the curvy blonde of a cartoon serial, Jane. Her mildly catastrophic adventures always took place either just as she was starting to put her clothes on or just before she had finished taking them all off. The *Daily Mirror* attracted a readership for whom the established dailies were too sophisticated, too anti-Labour or, as was the case with the *Daily Herald*, dull. The *Daily Sketch* was provoked by the *Daily Mirror*'s new policy to banner its contents with the haughty assertion, 'All the News That Is Fit to Print'. The result was that by 1938 the *Daily Sketch* had lost 183,000 readers and the *Daily Mirror* had gained 300,000. Significantly in a paper that was to go on to capture a large part of the working-class market, the *Daily Mirror* never viewed society as complacently as the *Daily Express* and soon combined cheesecake with a calculatedly plebeian radicalism.

The English were better served by their national dailies than they realized. No publication save one, the Communist *Daily*

Worker (which was founded in 1930, sold only 100,000 copies and was rechristened *Morning Star* in 1966), derived its finances wholly from a political party. And such was the wealth and the individualism of the much-abused 'Press lords' that nobody could afford to bribe them as those who ran many continental newspapers were bribed by Nazis and Fascists. Beaverbrook was so individualistic that he allowed the New Zealand-born cartoonist, Low, to produce night after night in the *Evening Standard* political cartoons wholly opposed to the whole drift of the Beaverbrook policy. Much contemporary hostility to the popular Press derived from the intellectual snobbery that disliked any attempt to cater for the lower orders in the field of journalism equally with attempts to provide them with entertainment through film, radio and popular music. If the popular Press failed to impress on its readers the reality either of the menace of Hitler or the scandal of unemployment it was a fault it shared with the bulk of the quality Press and most of the politicians.

For the formation of serious opinion the educated turned to the weekly periodicals. The 'quality' Sundays then had small circulations, though the *Observer* attracted notice through the elephantine prose of its Editor and leader writer, J. L. Garvin, the nearest thing the period produced to a thundering journalist of the nineteenth-century variety. The effective political weeklies were *Time and Tide* which had a strong feminist twist under its owner and Editor, Lady Rhondda, the then rather stodgily Conservative *Spectator* and the *New Statesman and Nation* which, during the 30 years starting in 1931, was edited by Kingsley Martin, a progressive Socialist of the most enlightened kind and with a delight in prophesying disaster in every issue. It was the established organ of the intellectual left wing, and this, together with its *avant-garde* literary and other reviews, made it one of the thirties' most influential journals.

The mass circulation of the Press, the banning of commercial radio and the limitations placed on the use of hoardings, particularly in the countryside, gave to the newspaper advertisement the place in the popular mind occupied in the 1960s by the television commercial. The absence of colour likewise tended

to make Press advertising predominantly verbal; and even in the
thirties posters seemed still unable
to make their point without a
slogan. The most effective of the
many lively posters of A. W. Hassall
was remembered for its slogan,
'Skegness is So Bracing', rather
than for its jolly prancing fisher-
man. The period was thus rich
in catchwords. The advertisers
themselves had their catchphrase:
'Swear not by the moon, th'incon-
stant moon, but by Constant
Advertising', but the most universal slogan was perhaps the simple
'Players Please' which insinuated
itself (and Player's cigarettes) into
everybody's awareness. Early in
the twenties a campaign to sell
seedless raisins in packets tempor-
arily universalized the question
'Have you had your iron today?'

*The slogan of this poster by A. W. Hassall
was one of the most enduring of the period. For
its later consequences, see page 164*

The age was very susceptible to the scientific approach to the sale
of articles of food. The phrase 'Keep That Schoolgirl Complexion'
sold soap as well as enriching the vernacular. So did the campaign to sell Kruschen Salts, of which a daily dose 'as much as
will cover a sixpence' was enough to turn arthritic old men into

Palmolive's ubiquitous slogan as used in the early twenties

stile-leaping athletes. By the thirties it was difficult to say 'Friday night' without somebody completing the sentence with 'is Amami night' since Friday was no longer 'bath night' but the evening when all women used Amami shampoo. And did the expression 'that sinking feeling' exist before the advertisements appeared to assert that Bovril prevented it?

The most significant phrase of the time was 'Delivered in a Plain Van'. This figured in the Press campaign run by 'Mr Drage' to persuade people to buy furniture on hire purchase or as it was disapprovingly called 'the never-never'. Delivery in a 'plain van' was designed to spare Drage's customers the embarrassment they might feel in those innocent days if their neighbours suspected them of having furniture in their house that they had not paid cash for. Mr Drage and his Plain Van played a major role in the creation of the hire-purchase habit though, even by 1939, it was still slightly suspect.

Further Reading

For the Press, Francis Williams, *Dangerous Estate*, 1957. For advertising, see E. S. Turner, *Shocking History of Advertising*, revised edition, 1965, Chapter 7. Incomplete references to reading habits are scattered through Mowat, *op. cit.*, Seaman, *op. cit.*, and Taylor, *op. cit.* Most books about reading matter are about 'literature' or about what intellectuals wrote and read, and therefore little related to the life of the time. Books on non-highbrow reading matter merely deplored it.

VIII

A People on Wheels

The great increase in the number of motor vehicles during the period both illustrated and encouraged the rising living standards of the time. There were just under 150,000 licensed motor vehicles in 1910; in 1920 there were 650,000; in 1930, 1·5 million; and by the outbreak of war the figure exceeded 3 million. The number of private cars rose from just over 300,000 in the early twenties to almost 2 million by 1938. Not only did the production of cars, buses, lorries, coaches and vans create a new industry; it created new skills, transformed the urban and rural landscapes and revolutionized the way of life of a great part of the population.

The decisive step forward was the adoption by the British car industry, though on a smaller scale, of the mass-production methods used by Henry Ford in the USA for the manufacture

Ascot Races, 1920. A solid tyred, open top B type London bus, an open charabanc and a lordly Rolls. The 'democratizing' effects of the internal combustion engine are already apparent

A picnic at Brooklands Motor Races, Easter 1923. The sun's rays light up the gleaming bodywork of a selection of family tourers parked on the grass in amiable informality

of his T-model. Although this Ford 'Tin Lizzie' was available in England, it was outdone in popular favour by the Morris family cars and, from 1924, by the first of the Baby Austins and subsequently by the early Morris Minor. The car ceased, in function, in method of production and in design, to be the rich man's horseless carriage it had chiefly been before 1914. As the twenties proceeded it was less and less a symbol of sophistication and extravagance, and such names as Hispano Suisa and Bentley, though esteemed to the point of idolatry both then and afterwards, belonged socially, even in their hey-day, to a departing world of privilege. It was the family tourer that changed society. It meant above all the popularization of leisured luxury; it was not widely used for commuting but mainly for evening and week-end jaunts and for holidays. Together with its humbler relative, the motor-cycle, it produced a whole new generation of amateur mechanics at precisely the time when sensitive people were bemoaning the repetitive character of modern man's working life and the decline of handicrafts. The masses, just when intellectuals insisted on see-ing them as mindless victims of the machine, cranked their engines with their starting-handles, sounded their jub-ilant klaxons and, spurred on by the excited squeals of their children, the envious gaze of neighbours and the agitated tremors of their wives, drove off for a day in the country or down to the sea. For the younger generation, motor-cycle and secondhand car or sports car provided oppor-tunities for displays of dash and bravado just when it had been decided that in-dustrialization had con-demned them to lives of total monotony. The boy on a motor-bike, with or without a girl on the flapper bracket, and the bescarved undergraduate flouting proctorial regula-tions by driving an MG sports or bull-nosed Morris at speed, were character-istic figures of the time.

Nor did sensitive souls seeking to resuscitate an-tique rural folk-songs (suit-ably bowdlerized) or yearn-ing once again to see morris dancers instead of Morris Minors hard by the village green observe that the new age was already producing legends and cults of its

Australian cricketers and British cars. Clarry Grimmett, legendary spin bowler and W. H. Ponsford, stolid opener, study the latest models at the Morris Motor Works, Cowley, Oxford, 1926

6-cylinder 27 h.p. Hispano-Suiza with coachwork by Weymann, 1929 or 1930, illustrates the survival of the grand manner

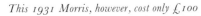

This 1931 Morris, however, cost only £100

'B. Bira' wins the Nuffield Trophy at Donnington in his E.R.A. 'Hanuman', 1939

own. Grand Prix motor-racing could only be seen abroad and Brooklands was the only place in England where motor-racing was legal until a road-racing circuit was opened at Donington Park in 1933; nevertheless, Sir Henry Segrave in a Sunbeam was, in 1927, the first man to exceed 200 mph, and was succeeded as holder of the land-speed record by Sir Malcolm Campbell and John Cobb, also using British-built cars. And if, in the thirties, the dynamic Fascist and Nazi drive for international prestige ensured the dominance of Grand Prix racing by Alfa Romeo and Mercedes Benz, the German teams (unlike the Italian) relied heavily on foreign drivers. One of them was the Englishman, Dick Seaman, a leading Grand Prix driver of 1938. From 1934 to 1939 the junior form of Grand Prix racing for 'light cars' or voiturettes (forerunners of the postwar Formula 2 racing-cars) was dominated by ERA (English Racing Automobiles), using what was basically a six-cylinder Riley engine. ERAs were driven by such memorable personalities as Raymond Mays and Prince Birabongse of Siam, who raced as 'B. Bira'.

3,300 c.c. Bugatti of 1939

Matching the growth of private transport was the expansion of public transport. Cars and motor-bikes were still relative luxuries or youthful extravagances; for getting to and from work, the shops and entertainments, for visits to friends and near-by towns and countryside, the motor-bus gradually became the dominant vehicle, outdating the tram much as the cinema outdated the music-hall. The monopoly by the bus of the main thoroughfares of the City and West End of London, where the busiest routes ran to a one- to two-minute frequency, was, however, a result of the historical accident that as far back as 1872 a veto had been imposed on the construction of tramways in central London. In the country as a whole, though the number of trams increased during the twenties to a peak figure of 14,500, operating on 2,600 miles of route and carrying between 4 and 5 million passengers a year, a Royal Commission pronounced a death-sentence in 1931. It recommended that no more tramways be constructed and that existing ones be gradually eliminated. The number of trams halved during the thirties and speedy extinction was postponed only by the outbreak of war. Typical of the process was a rise in bus passengers in Birmingham from 43 to 225 million a year in the thirties, with tram passengers dropping from 238 to 174 million.

In its day the tram had great advantages. It could accommodate up to 80 passengers. Until the twenties it was more

Buses in Oxford Street about 1927

Trams at Cross Lane Junction, Salford, 1939. A spider's web of wires, a jangle of points, and it is raining. The typical townscape within which the trams operated

reliable than the motor-bus and had very cheap fares, including workmen's fares at a halfpenny a mile, all roughly the same in 1938 as in 1908. This put up running costs and represented a heavy burden on local rates, since most tramways were owned municipally. Although Leeds and Liverpool extended their routes in the thirties and Blackpool and London produced trams of modern design, most trams were by now getting old and noisy. 'There is', wrote J. B. Priestley, 'something depressing about the way in which a tram lumbers and grinds along like a sick elephant.' Their routes were restricted to the old inner suburbs, so that the outward expansion of suburbia inevitably led to bus routes running from the perimeter of the town right to the centre; tram-tracks in the centre of the road were a hazard to passengers getting on or off and a source of irritation and delay to motor vehicles. The rails were deadly for cyclists, who skidded on them in wet weather. Always somewhat proletarian, the tram became synonymous with drab industrial streets, decaying inner suburbs, its once uniquely brilliant electric lights outshone by bright street lamps and the garish neon signs of modernity.

Tramways had provided a useful day-time load for the municipal electric power-stations. This factor, together with the new electricity boom of the thirties, explains the move to replace trams by trolley-buses which, though not confined to a track and thus able to draw in to the kerb to collect and drop passengers, still drew on electric power through overhead wires. Leeds, in 1891 the first town to introduce electric trams using overhead wires, was in 1911, along with Bradford, the first to use trolley-buses. They were introduced in Birmingham in 1922 and in the London area in 1931. At its best the trolley-bus was not only the most handsome of public service vehicles, but the quietest and most comfortable. Its general supersession after a relatively short reign, by the all-conquering diesel-fuelled bus, was a technologically retrograde step, due to faulty transport economics and the anti-social explosion of private motoring in cities in the years after 1951.

The motor-bus both responded to and stimulated the outward suburban growth of towns, and in the rural areas effectively ended the isolation of all but the remotest hamlets. The life of most villages within a 20-mile radius of any reasonably prosperous town was liable to be revolutionized by the transport developments of the time. The decline of the landowner, the low profits of agriculture and the appallingly low wages of agricultural workers tended to turn many villages in southern England within convenient motoring distance of a sizeable town into a kind of rural suburb beyond the suburbs. The squire had gone, and so had most of the young people; their place was taken by middle-class

Trolleybus

'residents'. Ownership of car and telephone (and a wireless set for the winter evenings), the existence of a bus service and an electricity supply, the readiness of tradesmen to send goods by van and the hope, if not the fact, of main drainage made it possible for the first time for people born and bred in towns to live in the country. For these new 'villagers' the land was no longer something to be worked; it was scenery to be looked at. It also had to be 'preserved'—chiefly against any further new-comers, since the result would be to spoil the 'character' of 'their' village. Indeed, where such exclusiveness failed to operate, and where the quality of the land was poor in the first instance, the consequences were disastrous. Great stretches of land in south Essex, with their easy access from east London and to the sea at Clacton or Southend, became a riotous disorder of wooden and asbestos shacks used both for week-ends and as permanent homes. They were often put up by their owners themselves, testifying at once to aesthetic insensitiveness and unquenchable individualism.

The long-distance coach also linked village with town, and town with town. In its first, roofless form, it was known in print as a 'charabanc' and in common speech as a 'sharrabang' or 'sharra', and replaced the traditional horse 'brake' for outings to the country. As an enclosed motor-coach it also brought the petrol engine into competition with the railways: a regular service between Bristol and London opened early in the twenties, and by the thirties coaches provided a markedly cheaper alter-native to the railway, both for the mass holiday traffic and for journeys between major cities. Long-distance coach travel, besides being cheaper, guaranteed a seat with every advance booking; the up-and-over-the-bridge traipsing, the hugger-mugger standing in the corridor, the almost insuperable prob-lem of getting anything eatable to eat, the atmosphere of Victorian gloom and dinginess associated with the majority of railway stations, all helped to divert traffic to the motor-coach. In the thirties, the railways campaigned for Government assis-tance, displaying posters asking for 'A Square Deal for the Railways'. Crack trains alone preserved railway prestige, though failing to halt the deterioration of railway finance. The

LNER's Silver Jubilee to Newcastle, the Coronation Scot and Sir Nigel Gresley's Pacific locomotives made record-breaking runs; but these and the dignified expresses on the Great Western and the south-western section of Southern apart, the railways were energetically grumbled about long before they were nationalized in 1948.

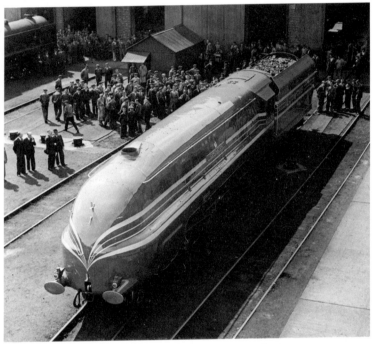

The streamlined LMS locomotive, 'Coronation Scot', 1937

The delivery-van and lorry also took traffic from the railways and it could be argued that it was the internal combustion engine that defeated the General Strike by proving that the belief that the nation's economic life could not function if denied coal and steam-power was already outdated. The commercial vehicle also hastened the process by which the use of the horse was slowly confined to its historic one of encouraging gambling, or for getting little girls into jodhpurs; its agricultural use, however, continued throughout the period, for there was relatively little mechanization on the farm as yet. The coal-man, the milkman, the brewer and the rag-and-bone man were becoming the last major users of the horse in urban streets; coal was bought weekly or casually by the hundredweight sack in most parts, and milkmen rode their 'floats', standing behind their churns rather like charioteers, delivering to their customers twice daily.

The internal combustion engine substituted petrol fumes for horse droppings as the principal hygienic hazard of urban streets and was rather unjustly regarded as if it had invented the traffic jam, though as far back as the 1850s commuters had been complaining that it took less time to travel from Brighton to London Bridge by train than to get from London Bridge to Paddington by cab, on account of the traffic congestion. In the countryside, however, the petrol engine ended for good the long Victorian peace created on the roads by the railway's monopoly of all but the lightest traffic. As well as the frustrations of con-gestion there were the dangers resulting from the streak of anarchic individualism engendered in most males when first placed behind a steering-wheel. At the beginning of the twenties even buses had no fixed stops. The authorities sought to restrict danger to life and limb by a speed-limit of 20 mph until 1930, thus ensuring that, in addition to showing contempt for other human beings, motorists should also regard themselves as bucca-neers at war with lawful authority. The 'road hog' was a much abused figure. Gradually, the anti-motoring prejudices of elderly magistrates proving inadequate to the task of bringing order out of chaos, environmental regimentation and highway engineering began their never-succeeding effort to facilitate and yet regulate the increasing flow of vehicles. Arterial roads, by-passes, traffic lights, one-way streets, roundabouts and pedes-trian crossings, a 30 mph speed-limit in built-up areas, together with a compulsory driving test, had all been brought into use by 1934. The last three reforms were the work of Leslie Hore-Belisha, Minister of Transport in the National Government; he gave his name to Belisha beacons. The result, though disfiguring to both town and country, was greatly to reduce road accidents which, in proportion to the number of vehicles, were far greater before 1934 than they have been since. The size of the traffic problem even in the thirties may be judged by the fact that, in the three days of the August Bank Holiday of 1935, 37,943 cars, coaches and motor-cycles entered Blackpool.

All road-users were inclined to blame both accidents and congestion on the country's inadequate roads; but the cautious and elderly minded conservatives who dominated the political parties and the civil service at the time regarded the internal combustion engine rather as cavalry officers regarded the tank. They disapproved of an invention that downgraded the horse and upgraded engineers and mechanics. The car, the bus and the motor-coach clogged the streets, fouled the air, turned village streets into race-tracks and filled village pubs with raucous charabanc-trippers every Saturday and Sunday night. As late as the Second World War Vita Sackville-West was bitterly upset to learn that a bus service was to pass close by her beloved garden at Sissinghurst. The spectacle of the lower classes spilling themselves all over rural England and giving rise to a rash of hideous petrol stations caused the popular intellectual of the thirties, C. E. M. Joad, later a BBC Brains Trust performer, to say of his contemporaries that they 'found England a land of beauty and left it a land of beauty-spots' (littered, he could have said, with ice-cream wrappings and empty bottles). Another writer quoted with approval the hostile comment of a German observer that in the south of England the land was no longer worked by families; the sons were manning petrol pumps and the daughters working as waitresses in roadside cafés.

Since road-making cost money and interfered with property rights, it had historically been the typical activity of dictators. History repeated itself in the thirties: for military reasons and for the sheer love of ostentatious prestige that went into their encouragement of Grand Prix automobiles, Hitler and Musso-lini were great road-builders. But public-works programmes of this sort were alien to the English politician; it is significant that Lloyd George who, in 1909, had invented the Road Fund that Churchill 'raided' in the twenties, was the only statesman to advocate large-scale road-building (as well as railway electrification). Roads were built, all the same. Apart from the Mersey road tunnel, completed in 1928, most of them were in the south; though even here it was characteristic that work on Western Avenue (later part of the A40) into London, already begun before 1914, was halted throughout the twenties. The Great West Road was finished in 1925, the North Circular, the Kingston and Watford by-passes a little later. Other improvements reshaped the routes to Dover, Brighton and Southend. Too many of the new arterial roads were of three-lane capacity only, and almost all were promptly beribboned with new houses or light factories, the Great West Road being the prototype in this respect. A feature of arterial roads leading to the south coast from London was the 'road house', with a dance-floor, restaurant and swimming-pool. Road houses were considered very expensive, very sophisticated and probably immoral. The visual aspect of the new roads was stark when compared with the traditional rolling English road; the highway engineering was cheeseparingly unimaginative; the roads' relatively big-scale and functional ruthlessness seemed inappropriate to the small-scale cosiness of the English landscape. Yet not all by-pass architecture was bad. Some of the new factories were honestly contemporary and without the fraudulent sentimentality of Victorian Gothic, speculative builders' mock-Tudor or the empty pomposity of joint-stock-bank Classicism.

The progressive railway developments of the time were the electrification of the Southern and the extension of the London Underground. Southern Electric reached Brighton in 1933, Hastings in 1935, Portsmouth in 1937 and Reading and Maidstone in 1939. Nothing Southern could do, however, could solve the eternal troubles of its lines to north Kent. Possibly the most uninterruptedly prosperous and expanding region of twentieth-century England, it attracted population to such places as Sidcup, Eltham and Bexley so continuously that throughout the thirties season-ticket holders living there (they were not called 'commuters' before 1939) rarely got seats in the rush hour and created unspeakable chaos night and morning at London Bridge as they herded themselves from one platform to the other trying

Chiswick Park station, west London, before rebuilding

to transfer themselves, from trains bound for (or starting from) Cannon Street, into trains to or from Charing Cross, and vice versa.

London's tube trains burrowed their way up and out of the London clay into the fields of Middlesex and Essex, creating vast new suburbs, just as Southern Electric turned villages into dormitory towns. The Hampstead line reached out from Golders Green to Edgware in 1924, the City and South London line from Clapham down to Morden in 1926. The Piccadilly tube went on from Finsbury to Cockfosters and westwards from Hammersmith to Uxbridge and Hounslow. The District reached

Chiswick Park station as rebuilt by London Transport, 1933. Simplicity and clean lines were the aim of 'modern' design in the thirties

out to far Becontree at Upminster in 1932. The Bakerloo created a whole new line for itself from Baker Street to Stanmore in 1939. All the areas into which these tube extensions penetrated were transformed from fields and villages into sprawling suburbs in little more than a decade, so that they are, in the design of their houses, shopping parades, pubs and cinemas, almost wholly of the 1930s. In some respects, however, electrification, both on the Southern and on the new tubes, like the adoption of the trolley-bus but unlike any changes accounted for by the petrol engine, improved the urban landscape. The newer tube trains and modernized stations of London Transport were exceptionally satisfying to the eye. The Southern's newer stations also used the longitudinal concrete style of the thirties less oppressively than some more ambitious efforts in this manner. London Transport, quite apart from its architecture, set an aesthetic standard in such matters as posters and street signs which deplorably few other public or private undertakings troubled to emulate.

The pioneer of all this development had, appropriately, been the Metropolitan, the first and once the most ambitious and far-flung of London's underground lines. Already by 1918 it ran electric trains to Harrow and steam-trains to Aylesbury. In 1925 the line was electrified to Rickmansworth, and the whole of this area had acquired the name 'Metroland'. To persuade people to buy houses in these rural parts, the Metropolitan was still enticing people in the 1920s with advertisements showing, in John Betjeman's words, 'sepia views of leafy lanes in Pinner'. The development of this and the other tube lines extended the built-up area of London so dramatically that Betjeman was soon to mourn that only 'a few surviving hedges keep alive our lost Elysium—rural Middlesex again'. It was already impossible by 1939 to believe with the same poet that as recently as the mid twenties

> Parish of enormous hayfields
> Perivale stood all alone
> And from Greenford scent of mayfields
> Most enticingly was blown.

Building in this north-western area was greatly stimulated by the holding of the British Empire Exhibition of 1924 and 1925 at Wembley, at which time the tram terminus at near-by Sudbury still marked the extreme outer edge of London.

The effect was that, all through the thirties, all who could afford it migrated from declining inner suburbs like Paddington and Shepherd's Bush to newly built houses in such places as Kenton and Kingsbury. To the east there was a similar migration from East Ham, Plaistow and Barking into Essex, greatly encouraged by Ford's new Dagenham Works and by the huge LCC housing estate at Becontree.

Further Reading

Books about transport tend to be highly technical or else the work of fanatics with little sense of history. Exceptionally in a popular work, J. Joyce, *Tramway Heyday*, 1964, neatly sets the tram in its social context. If and when Professor T. C. Barker and Michael Robbins produce volume II of their *History of London Transport*, of which volume I stops in 1900, fanatics and historians will alike rejoice. Various booklets are published from time to time by London Transport. For motor-racing, see Rodney Walkerley, *Automobile Racing*, 1962.

IX

Home and Away

A large part of the population was badly housed in 1919. In that year, partly owing to the suspension of building from 1914 to 1918, there were 610,000 fewer houses than families. In the next 20 years nearly 2·5 million private-enterprise houses and just over 1·5 million council houses were built; and in 1939 there were over 500,000 more houses than there were families. The excess of larger houses by 1939 was because families were smaller and servants rarer and more expensive; and there was an excess of smaller houses because of the poverty of unskilled workers and the unemployed, and the natural immobility of the many who lived in fairly poor-quality housing for which they paid very low rents as a result of rent control, which had existed since 1915. Moreover, only about 300,000 new houses had been built under slum-clearance schemes. There was an excess of houses by 1939; but there was still an excess of slums, and one calculation was that the total of sub-standard houses in England and Wales was as high as a million.

Acts to subsidize the building of houses by local authorities to be let at less than the economic rent were passed in 1919, 1923 and 1924. Slum-clearance Acts were passed in 1930 and 1933, but private-enterprise house-building predominated during the thirties. All three types of building changed both the physical appearance of England and the social habits of English people. The new house-building programmes depended on the public transport facilities that now enabled towns to spread outwards while still linking homes on new estates with traditional places of work in city centres; they were also a stimulus to the electricity industry, the distributive trades and the consumer-goods industries.

The object of subsidized council-house building was to overcome the inability of private enterprise to make a profit out of building houses to let at very low rents. The urban slums inherited from the Victorian era had been created by the simple fact that their occupiers could afford to rent no more than the barest minimum of accommodation and were compelled by their poverty to live within walking distance of their place of work. Industrial Scotland had working-class accommodation of a notoriously low standard. But by 1919 it had long been apparent that bad housing caused ill health and unsocial habits. The very poor had houses which resembled those of many of the somewhat better-off in having no bathrooms, but were in even worse plight in lacking water-closets and sometimes even a cold-water tap of their own. They had neither gardens nor fuel-stores and if the family were large they had at best two bedrooms for all of them. They suffered disproportionately from tuberculosis and bronchitis, their rates of infant mortality were four times those of the more prosperous; and the disparaging phrase that

Limehouse Causeway, East London, 1925. The cloak and bonnet worn by elderly women and widows of the time. The scene harks back to the days of Sherlock Holmes

London slums of the early twenties

described the poor as 'the great unwashed' spelled out the significant fact referred to by J. B. Priestley, when he once wrote that one of the major differences that came over the working classes in the twentieth century was that as time went on they ceased any longer to be recognizable simply by their smell.

Council housing was thus seen as a beneficent operation in social hygiene. Many council-house estates, perhaps designed by planners who knew their Patrick Geddes and Ebenezer Howard, were designed as groups of cottages round little imitation cathedral closes or pocket-sized village greens, like parts of a poor people's Welwyn Garden City. It was mandatory that council houses have bathrooms; and in view of their absence from many people's homes in the twenties, this excited hostile comment. 'These people' would keep their coals in their bath and would, because of their deplorable habits, turn their new houses into slums almost immediately. This *rus in urbe* atmosphere was illustrated by the Wythenshawe housing estate outside Manchester, built between 1925 and 1934 and, on a small scale, at East Acton, in west London, built under the 1919 Act.

Many authorities, however, built their council houses on extensive estates, well away from town centres or, as was the case with Leeds and several London estates, for example, remote from them. The immediate effect of these long rows of small houses, often semi-detached and finished in roughcast, was monotonous and characterless, partly because of the lack of high buildings or public buildings of any sort, or even of pleasant green circuses at intersections. The bleakness was eventually mollified by the flowers and foliage of the tiny gardens attached to each house; but the segregation of so many working-class households inside council estates well away both from town centres and from the rest of the community tended, like the educational segregation of the time, to make contemporary references to the disappearance of class differences somewhat superficial.

Nor was removal to a council estate always an unmixed blessing. Rents were usually higher and fares to work cost more, so that the health of both mothers and children might decline in consequence of there being less money to spend on food. From a social point of view, council housing also helped to immobilize the country's labour force, since councils rented their houses only to applicants at the top of a long waiting-list of their own citizens. To take a job in a different town could well mean waiting indefinitely for another council house.

If council houses were resented, the private-enterprise houses of the time were despised (and bungalows were considered so

Wythenshawe council estate near Manchester in the thirties

The less ambitious type of private enterprise housing of the twenties and thirties. Casement, but not metal, windows, roughcast, red tiles, and still terraced

especially hideous that it was common form to speak of 'bungaloid growths'). The cheaper ones were considered architecturally deplorable and described, unjustifiably, as jerry-built. Sometimes they were criticized for being monotonously alike, mostly when built on peripheral suburban estates without public or social amenities; this in due time led to estate agents saying of a house they had to sell, 'not on an estate'. Sometimes they were criticized for not being alike. Basically a square box, each house tended to disguise the fact with unnecessary gables, pebbledash, leaded panes (considered very superior) or mock-Tudor timbering. Clough Williams-Ellis affected to distinguish two predominant styles which he amusingly labelled 'Early Twirly' and 'Late Straight'. Osbert Sitwell predicted with confident inaccuracy that they would 'inevitably become the slums of the future'. Inordinate contempt was expressed by all cultivated persons for the passion for semi-detached houses. There was still much new building of terraced houses; but they came to be thought so greatly inferior to semi-detached houses that when terraced houses were again put on the market in the 1960s, house agents had to disguise them by calling them 'town houses', preferably with the epithet 'Georgian'. This was a shrewd recognition of the fact that the revulsion from the terraced house in the thirties was a revulsion from the Victorian terraced house in which in all probability most buyers of the new semis had first seen the light of day (but never at any time very much of it).

Most contemporary criticism of council houses and private-enterprise semis reflected the smug snobbishness of persons who had never had to live in the kind of house from which the new homes provided a blessed release. The typical Late Victorian and Edwardian small terraced house was dark, narrow and poky. It had a six-foot-long garden path at the front, which meant there was a front garden in which nothing could grow once a dreary little privet hedge had been planted. It had a long dark passage leading to a long dark kitchen and beyond it there was a small cold scullery. Off the passage was a front room, and behind

Mock Tudor beams and decorative twiddles indicate rather more expensive houses

that a second sitting-room from which most of the light was excluded by the kitchen and scullery extending beyond it into the back garden. There was no bathroom, illumination was by gas and there was an outside lavatory. The narrowness of the house reduced the width of the back garden to that of a chicken run, giving an uninterrupted view of similar chicken-run gardens to left and right and beyond.

There was no hot-water system, and all washing, culinary and personal alike, was done at the kitchen sink. When the weekly bath was taken it was done in the kitchen in a zinc bath brought in from the nail in the wall outside the back door on which it normally hung. Cooking, heating and the boiling of water were done on the kitchen range, a cast-iron construction consisting of a fire-grate with a hob on top and an oven to the side of it. The old terraced house meant mothers kneeling down and beseeching, coaxing or cussing the kitchen-range fire to 'draw' in order to get the oven hot or, on washing day, bending over the scullery 'copper' full of hot water (boiled in kettles on the range), heaving out the sheets with a copper-stick, rubbing shirts drastically with bar soap on a scrubbing-board, transferring them in great bowls to the mangle, turning its great handle as if winding a mighty windlass and then

Miner washes himself in a zinc bath in front of the kitchen range

151

*The Clinical Style of interior decoration shown in idealised form,
1936, with concealed lights, built-in electric heating, standard
lamp, hand-tufted carpet, folk-weave curtains, and neutral walls
devoid of wallpaper or pictures*

ironing the lot with a weighty flat-iron, also heated on the range. The old terraced house symbolized the days when married women without servants were manual labourers. The new women could not get servants and had no intention of being the female navvies their mothers had been. The clever sniggerers at the suburban semis, such as the Sitwells and Waughs, whose mothers had left all this domestic manual labour to the servants, were unaware of these simple truths.

The typical house of the thirties would have a tiled roof instead of nineteenth-century slate, and by being square and semi-detached had a wider garden—though not necessarily very wide, since the detachment of a semi from the house to which it was not detached was often so slight that a street of such houses looked a little like a row of rather widely spaced teeth. But the gap was wide enough to allow access at the side for the delivery of coal, which in terraced houses had to be carried through the house to the coalshed at the back if there were no back alleyway. Bicycle or motor-bike could also be got to and from the back of the house without having to be taken through the old hall passage. Only the more expensive semis had garages, however. The land prices in the outer areas permitted a larger front garden as well as the squarer back garden, thus providing better opportunity of planting for privacy.

The ground-plan would offer two living-rooms, which were increasingly described as 'dining-room' and 'lounge' respectively. The word 'lounge' replaced the older and more accurate 'sitting-room' and was socially superior to 'parlour', which was thought to be associated chiefly with working-class front rooms in Lancashire. The alternative, 'drawing-room', was dropped as being too reminiscent of cluttered Victorian interiors. By the thirties, kitchens tended to become 'kitchenettes' with, it was usually said, not enough room to swing a cat. This reduction in size was dependent on the steady decline in the use of kitchen ranges (and the consequent elimination of the old filthy chore of the weekly black-leading), in favour of gas or electric cookers, gas and electric water-heaters and the adoption of hot-water systems based on kitchen boilers fired by coke or anthracite. In the rather more expensive houses there was a hatch between kitchen and dining-room. This did not, as has several times been wrongly suggested, mean that the household expected to have a maid waiting on the other side of the hatch; it was a prized feature since it reduced the amount of fetching and carrying between the two rooms which was now necessary because there were no servants.

Crittall advertisement of 1928 (and later) with house of 'ultra-modern' design

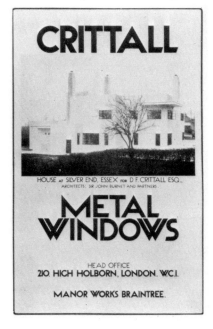

Upstairs were three bedrooms, the third likely to measure little more than eight feet by six, a bathroom and lavatory, combined or separate. The daintily described 'low flush suite' was beginning to replace the traditional 'ball and chain', but still aroused a certain mistrust. All the rooms in the house were by any standards small, but this was made less obvious by the greatly increased

153

daylight that reached them as a result of the introduction of metal windows. The name of Crittall (metal windows) like Ascot and Sadia (gas and electric water-heaters respectively) and Jackson (electric cookers) and, of course, Hoover, all symbolized the domestic revolution of the thirties. The enterprise of the electricity industry led to the disappearance of the fragile gas-mantle and its 'by-pass' in favour of the electric light bulb; and it at last made internal light functional by way of the standard lamp, a much-derided feature of the new suburbia, partly on account of the enormous and sometimes grossly fringed shades that were used. Electricity could also compensate in part for the absence of central heating, by means of portable electric fires. These caused superior people to smirk when they took the form of imitation coal or log fires and to wince when functionally and adventurously designed in chrome. More expensive homes had still newer developments, as described in *The Studio's Yearbook of Decorative Art* for 1933:

> Glass and metal are very popular, and every year they are put to new and attractive use. Mirror glass, in particular, used with discretion, is decoratively effective and adds to the feeling of space. Perhaps the most striking development is in the use of electric light. Although its primary function is to illuminate, its possibilities as a decorative element are being fully explored. In fact, the favoured form of lighting is the 'indirect' method—rows of lights, themselves concealed, but directed on to walls and ceiling from which the light is reflected. . . . Electric heating also takes its place as an important adjunct to the modern room. Set flush with the wall, it takes up no space, and . . . is thoroughly in keeping with modern schemes of decoration.

Electricity also provided the home with power-driven devices optimistically called 'labour-saving', though they were, more accurately, servant-replacing. Every other caller at a suburban front door, if not in search of new readers for one of the national dailies, was a vacuum-cleaner salesman; and a Hoover or Electrolux was the most coveted of domestic appliances. The electric iron replaced the flat-iron and, on Amami night, the absence of a lady's maid or 'the girl' to dry madam's hair was made up for by the electric hair-dryer. Washing-machines and refrigerators were also known to exist; but both were normally too expensive. Among the minor blessings of the time was the introduction of stainless-steel cutlery; this obviated the traditional chore of cleaning table knives frequently with knife-polish.

The total effect was to take domestic life in such houses out of the shadows and into the light and to make a home a source of pride without also being a cause of drudgery. Small rooms were made to seem larger by the fierce impatience of the new generation with dark brown paint, knick-knacks and glumly oppressive wallpaper. Pastel shades of distemper, topped by a paper frieze (often of painful design) under the picture-rail were preferred to wallpaper, paintwork was cream, yellow or apple-green, and pictures were either wholly banished or kept to a clinical minimum. Large furniture comprised the three-piece suite, the radio or radiogram, the standard lamp, a nest of tables, an overgrown hassock known as a 'pouffe' and a minimal bookcase. The piano, already more honoured in most homes for its presence than for its musical uses, was banished. The three-piece suite was deeply upholstered and sometimes glorified with 'jazzy' (i.e. erratically striped) loose covers. Dining-room furniture was most popularly of light or 'limed' oak. Ornaments were few, and likely to be limited to a dainty electric clock or a translucent glass figure of a young woman apparently straining upwards, either towards the shade of Isidora Duncan or towards an unattainably Utopian future. There would probably be a tiled fireplace, vaguely reflecting the ziggurat motif so frequent in the 1930s style, and replacing the traditional black fire-grate and its usually grimly elaborate mantelpiece.

Everything conspired to rationalize and simplify domestic ways and means in the new suburbs. The advent of branded goods, available at the new shopping parade round the corner, and the invasion of the High Street by the multiple stores, such as the International, David Greigs, Pearks and Macfisheries, made shopping simpler and more hygienic (it was the height of

Peter Jones department store, Sloane Square, London, completed 1939

modernity for anything to be wrapped in cellophane) and cooking less fundamental. In the same way, Burton's and the Fifty Shilling Tailor simplified the buying of clothes for men, and Woolworth's, Marks and Spencer and the British Home Stores simplified the buying of household and personal requisites in general. Custards, jellies, blancmange and porridge came for the first time out of packets and Viota mixture and Green's sponge mixture reduced some of the hazards of cakemaking. Breakfast cereals, notably Force, Grape Nuts and then Shredded Wheat, when allied with the electric toaster and coffee percolator, broke the breakfast-time monopoly of eggs and bacon, saved time and cooking and were, so it was proclaimed, healthier. The tin-opener, needed at the start of the period only when (as was usual) the opener provided with the sardine-tin broke off,

Stop Me and Buy One. Wall's had 8,500 of these ice cream tricycles on the road by 1939

was in constant use at the end, to deal with the tinned salmon and the tinned peaches. The passion for ice-cream, now much used as a ready-prepared 'sweet course', mounted year by year. In 1919 cornets and wafers were bought from street-vendors; by 1939, Wall's, previously famous for sausages, had created a widespread demand for the ice 'brick'. Wall's employed armies of cycling 'Stop Me and Buy One' salesmen, who propelled through highways and byways,

Kensal House, London W.10, 1936. Working class flats with nursery school. Built on the site of an old gasworks

miniature refrigerators, full of wrapped 'bricks' costing twopence each.

'Modern' though it all was, it was mostly still grounded in the very English tradition of the English country-house and garden, though its original inspiration was the red-brick Lutyens domestic style of the Edwardian period. Aesthetic persons found the new ubiquity of red brick unpleasant, failing to understand the equally strong distaste of the new suburbanite for the blackened, grey or peeling stuccoed houses amid which they had been brought up. Architects would have preferred them to live in concrete houses, which shouted their modernity far too blatantly (and were often banned by local councils) or in flats. Luxury flats, and blocks of council flats such as those at Kensal House in London or at Quarry Hill in Leeds, were indeed built and honoured in all the architectural books and journals of the time. But flats were wholly urban, were justifiably considered unsuitable for children, and also deprived their occupiers of the precious gardens that served to give them the assurance they so badly needed that they had escaped, at least when their daily work was over, from the invariably depressing urban environment in which they had been brought up. And so, strenuously, fanatically, the rough ex-meadow, littered with builders' rubble in front of the new house and behind it, was brought under cultivation and reduced to level lawn, flanking herbaceous borders and terminal vegetable patch. Rows upon rows of peas, beans and lettuces, and uncountable trenches of potatoes were optimistically planted; chrysanthemums were nervously pinched and stopped; dahlia tubers reverently lifted and stored. Michaelmas daisies, sunflowers, golden rod and lupins were religiously coaxed towards that brief flowering period which preceded the 11 remaining months of the year when their stalks and leaves were either hideous, dying or cut down. Fences disappeared behind rampant branches of rambler roses such as the uninspiringly pink Dorothy Perkins or the ugly red and white American Pillar. Hybrid tea roses flourished. Though they suffered from a regimen of obsessive over-pruning and the increasing rarity of horse manure, they had as yet little to fear from the still only nascent floribunda, and varieties such as Madame Butterfly, Ophelia, Picture, Shot Silk, Crimson Glory and President Hoover reigned supreme in catalogue and garden. No description of the domestic Englishman's leisure is valid that ignores the hours he spent (and not only if he lived in a semi) wielding lawn-mower, spade, fork, shears and secateurs.

If the new suburbia enabled more and more people lower down the social scale to ape their betters, it also, by allowing them to live comfortably without domestic servants, eliminated the one factor that most clearly marked them as 'not working class'. To have at least one servant was so essential a mark of respectability that in 1931 nearly one in every five households still had at least one full-time domestic living in; and the employment of a daily maid, complete with cap and apron, was not beyond the means of a grammar-school master who had paid off his mortgage or reached his maximum salary. Servants were increasingly difficult to get in the towns, above all in the south-east, but as late as 1939 a well-off family of three in the

West Country might employ a cook, a housemaid and a chauffeur-gardener; though it was a sign of the times in more ways than one if the cook and the housemaid were refugees from central Europe. Such English girls as were still available for domestic service proved either halfwittedly ignorant of the most elementary of domestic routines (a fact without which *Punch* would have been deprived of most of its jokes) or else likely to demand gramophones or wirelesses of their own, a prettily decorated bedroom and plenty of time off. The day when the female who called once a week to help with the rough work could refer to one of her friends as 'the lady who works for the woman next door to you' was not far off.

Prices for the new semis could be as low as from £300 to £500. A thousand pounds would buy a fair-sized architect-designed detached house with garage. The enterprise of the Building Societies, combined with 2 per cent Bank Rate, created a whole new race of owner-occupiers who secured their new homes by a down payment of around £25 and monthly payments over 25 years of £3–£4. These apparently small figures have to be set against the national average wage of £200 a year, against council-house rents of 7s.–15s. a week, against the less than 10s. a week rent paid by many long-term occupiers of quite well-preserved terraced houses subject to rent control, and against the fact that mortgages were rarely available to non-salaried workers.

New suburbs increased the sale not only of lawn-mowers but also tennis-rackets. By the early thirties, the answer to the celebrated question, 'Who's for tennis?' was 'Practically everybody' —or at least all who could afford a white tennis dress or white flannels and were willing to clean a pair of white gym-shoes. Subject to these limitations, tennis became the first nearly classless sport for both sexes, for clubs were attached to even quite humble churches and chapels and did a little to keep young people in attendance, at least during their time as courting couples or young marrieds. The tennis habit owed something to the glamour of Wimbledon stars such as the dashing Suzanne Lenglen or the formidable Bill Tilden and Fred Perry as well as the bravely never-quite-making-it Betty Nuttall and 'Bunny'

159

Alex James of Arsenal, in action against Preston North End

Austin. Mostly, however, it was the last stage in the democratization of the once purely middle-class tennis-party of the 1890s. In the case of men, tennis flourished without the support of schoolmasters, who disliked it as not being a team game. Schoolmasters did their best to use sport as a prop for old social habits. Association football was still therefore too proletarian to be practised at 'good' schools and most educated persons regarded the professional game, with its hired players and cloth-capped fans, with distaste. No intellectuals in those days analysed the skills of Alex James and no professors enthused over Arsenal as 30 years later their successors made a cult of Tottenham Hotspur, though even the most cursory reader of the sports news could hardly have been ignorant of Chelsea's abiding reputation as a side that was always comically incompetent. The steady increase in attendance at League games also produced the home-made cliché that the English were becoming a nation of spectators. Soccer was also looked down on because the bulk of the League teams, and almost all the most successful ones, belonged to the industrial parts of the country. Disapproval of soccer deepened with the advent of football pools in the thirties, for this added the sin of gambling to the sin of professionalism.

The Rugby Union game, wholly amateur, and with no competitive league table like soccer to put a premium on playing for victory, was deeply respected as thoroughly free from the taint of professionalism; players of the Rugby League game, being professionals, went unmentioned in the South in the way that before 1914 polite society ignored divorced women. The building of Wembley Stadium did something to moderate the dislike of football professionalism. Once the FA cup final was played regularly at Wembley (from 1923) the tradition was

The first Wembley Cup Final, 1923: the crowds overflow on to the pitch before the start of the game

established that the monarch himself presided over the event and presented the Cup to the winning team. Moreover, the Rugby League cup final was also played at Wembley, so that it secured at least one day's annual recognition in the metropolis.

Even cricket had its skeleton in the cupboard, in the form of League cricket, played in certain well-defined areas in Lancashire, Yorkshire and Staffordshire. This League system of one-day cricket on Saturdays, played by part-time players supporting one or two star professionals who were idols to their local fans, went as unreported outside its native haunts as if it had been American baseball. County cricket, by contrast, continued to inspire most schoolboys to hero-worship and to enable parsons and headmasters to make uplifting references to the Straight Bat, the One Great Scorer and to Playing the Game.

Jack Hobbs demonstrates the art of the straight bat for the benefit of London elementary schoolboys, 1934

It was also a cult among writers and poets and wrung prose poems out of reporters ('Woolley's bat, like a sundial, tells only the sunny hours'). It was an age of good wickets and frequent fine summers, and therefore of legendary batsmen, the best of whom might reasonably hope to score their first 1,000 runs before the end of May. The great names of the time were Hobbs and Sutcliffe, Woolley and Hendren, and after them Walter Hammond and the young Len Hutton; but such bowlers as Larwood, Verity and Maurice Tate elicited hardly less admiration. Cricket had its crises, of course. The worst was the bodyline controversy when the Australians claimed in 1932 that the English captain, D. R. Jardine, and the fast bowler, Larwood, had won the Test series by unfair tactics and complained at such a high diplomatic level that, when the Australians came to England in 1933, Larwood and his companion fast bowler, Voce, did not play against them.

Cricket retained its cachet because, in an age generally held to be becoming more and more democratic, it remained snobbish. Professionals formed the bulk of all county teams, though they had also to be qualified by birth or residence; but all teams were captained by amateurs, even if, in some cases, they were the kind of amateur who batted at number seven. These years were rich in many-initialled amateurs, most of them county or England captains: R. E. S. Wyatt, P. G. H. Fender, A. E. R. Gilligan, A. P. F. Chapman, J. W. H. T. Douglas and R. W. V. Robins; and Hampshire was captained by a real Lord. So sharp was the distinction between professionals and amateurs that they used separate dressing-rooms, and although newspapers ceased to report 'when Mr Fender joined Hobbs there was some lively running between the wickets' they adhered to the scorecard etiquette of giving amateurs their initials but recording professionals only by their surnames. It was the usual way of referring to servants. One of the highlights of the season was the annual game at Lord's between the amateurs and the professionals; no one thought it in the least offensive that the official title of the fixture was the Gentlemen *v.* Players match.

All three of the major ball games—association football, rugby football and cricket—were sustained by innumerable small local clubs, but suffered to some extent from their exclusively male character. Girls were licensed followers at rugger and cricket, but soccer was very much a man's world and none of these sports had the bisexual character of tennis. Nevertheless, a National Playing Fields Association was formed in the thirties in the hope of encouraging greater participation in the manly sports, since there had developed a slightly nervous fear lest the nation fail to 'Keep Fit'. It was noticeable that, whereas in the twenties the body had signified sex, in the thirties it signified healthy athleticism. In 1930 a Women's League of Health and Beauty was set up by a Miss Prunella Stack, and females of all ages were lured into lying *en masse* on floors and, attired in white satin blouses and white shorts, performing physical exercises in unison. They gave public displays of their prowess.

Also borrowed from the mass-conditioning physical-culture techniques of continental Fascism was the brief craze in the thirties for 'hiking'. Active people had been going on rambles in the country for years in a casual fashion; now they were encouraged to attire themselves in open-necked shirts and shorts, burden themselves with a huge pack, full of paraphernalia, and go off into the country in large communal droves. The Youth Hostel movement, launched in 1930, had rather different origins and, being grounded more deeply in affection for the countryside, proved more lasting.

Another attempt to regiment the race when at leisure was the vogue for community singing, a device which endured well into the Second World War. The most astonishing manifestation of this strange cult was organized at the Wembley Cup Final. Led by an expert in these matters, the crowd was kept singing in a marvellously docile fashion while waiting for the game to begin, and the conclusion was the mass singing of the hymn 'Abide

Skegness is SO Bracing: Butlin's first holiday camp opened there for the delight of these happy campers in 1937

With Me'. This entitled Cup Final Day to rank as one of the two major religious festivals of the English year; the other was Armistice Day, which featured the only other hymn that Englishmen all knew, 'O God Our Help in Ages Past'.

Two wholly urban pastimes were invented in the period, Speedway-racing and Greyhound-racing. The latter, like football pools, offered fresh outlets for the national passion for gambling. For a rather different social class, the steamship companies invented the summer cruise; but cruises, like more orthodox holidays abroad, were still for the very few. Despite the inception of Holidays with Pay in 1938, the normal holiday (if more could be afforded than an occasional day out) was the week or perhaps fortnight at a seaside boarding-house. In the early twenties it was still quite common for the landlady not to supply food for her lodgers, but merely to cook what the holiday-makers bought themselves from the local shops. By the end of the period it was usual to pay for full board; but already the seaside landlady of the traditional sort could no longer satisfy her more demanding patrons. Butlin's first holiday camp was opened at Skegness in 1937 and by the end of the period holiday camps had accommodation for half a million people. Nevertheless, of the 15 million who by the late thirties were estimated to be able to afford a week's holiday, most went to traditional south-coast resorts and to Margate and Southend. None of these could, of course, compete with Blackpool. On Bank Holiday Monday in August 1937 it had well over half a million visitors, arriving in 50,000 motor vehicles and 700 trains, 425 of them being specials, of which the first reached Blackpool at 3.55 a.m.; the last of such trains to leave Blackpool departed (for Sheffield) at 2.25 the following morning.

Further Reading

Two books on the urban landscape are Anthony Bertram, *Design*, a contemporary Pelican Special of 1938, and J. M. Richards, *An Introduction to Modern Architecture*. Bevis Hillier, *Art Deco*, 1968, offers an interesting analysis of the styles and themes of thirties' design. Osbert Sitwell, *Pillar to Post*, is supercilious about suburbia, John Betjeman, *Collected Poems*, 1962, often critical, but usually unmalicious and always evocative. For domestic service, see E. S. Turner, *What the Butler Saw*, 1962, Chapter 20. For an overall picture of housing policy and suburban development, see Mowat, *op. cit.*, pages 458–61, and Seaman, *op. cit.*, pages 236–8.

X
'What Do They Know of England. . .?'

After a Sunday afternoon spent amid 'the grim paraphernalia of industrialism' in the Midlands in 1933, J. B. Priestley was provoked to write in his *English Journey*:

> There ought to be no more of those lunches and dinners, at which political and financial and industrial gentlemen congratulate one another, until something is done about Rusty Lane and West Bromwich. While they still exist in their present foul shape, it is idle to congratulate ourselves about anything. They make the whole pomp of government here a miserable farce. . . . In the heart of the great empire on which the sun never sets, in the land of hope and glory, Mother of the Free, is Rusty Lane, West Bromwich. What do they know of England who only England know? The answer must be Rusty Lane, West Bromwich. And if there is another economic conference, let it meet there, in one of the warehouses, and be fed with bread and margarine and slabs of brawn. The delegates have seen one England, Mayfair in the season. Let them see another England next time, West Bromwich out of season. Out of all seasons except the winter of our discontent.

Ignorance about the realities of working-class life was indeed widespread among the rest of the population in 1933; and such knowledge as was disseminated about it by the end of the thirties sometimes obscured as much as it revealed. By 1939 it was hard to remember that not all the working class were permanently unemployed, that they did not all live in filthy slums and that England from Birmingham northwards was not in fact one continuous built-up area of back-to-back dwellings all occupied by families starving on the dole. Most respectable people of the period were, in relation to the working class, like the eighteenth-century bishop who, when asked what he thought of conditions in the Yorkshire woollen towns, replied that no gentleman ever went into the West Riding. In the 1920s, gentlemen did not often go into the East End either; and, in the days when it was just a street market like any other in London, neither did they go to the Portobello Road. Their knowledge of the urban poor came from pamphlets, social surveys and propaganda written by journalists in search of copy or left-wing or progressive do-gooders determined to make the comfortable middle class sup as full of horrors as possible. Even George Orwell's widely read studies, *Down and Out in Paris and London* and *The Road to Wigan Pier*, subtracted from knowledge as well as adding to it. Urban Lancashire was not all coal-mines and abysmal lodging-houses and neither were the working class or even the unemployed of London all engaged in a ceaseless tramp from doss-house to doss-house.

There were indeed differences between the working classes of the urban North and those of London. In the main, the North had a once-prospering (though never prosperous) working-class society that was slipping steadily into decay with no visible prospect of renewal. The working-class areas of London tended to reflect the poverty of those who had failed to get on and get out of them. If, in a sense, the North was like an industrial Portugal, left behind by the tides of change, the East End of London, except perhaps in traditional Dockland, was a sprawling transit camp, perpetually receiving its intake of poor immigrants and perpetually losing their abler children; while many of the lesser-known areas of poverty such as Battersea, North Paddington (and also Notting Hill, though not all of it) were areas of old middle-class family property transformed into makeshift flats for slightly more settled folk who could possibly expect to end their days living with son or daughter in one of the cheaper semis in a thirties-built suburb. Thus, the northern working class, though seeming to possess no certain future, had

167

Tyneside exterior, 1938

a more stable past and were the more tenacious in clinging to it. The descriptions of middle-aged people in the North to be found in Richard Hoggart's *The Uses of Literacy*, though written as late as 1957, are recognizably applicable to the working classes as they had been in the 1920s and 1930s in other parts of the country as well.

The outward appearance of working-class people once they were out of their teens differed radically from that of the better-off. The notion that cheap, mass-produced clothing had eradicated class differences may be disproved from any contemporary film or photograph. In the suburban South, by the late thirties, even grandmothers dressed (and felt) so young that they started to insist on being called 'Nana' (after the Darlings' dog?) instead of 'Gran'; but among the working class everywhere, a married woman began to be old at 25, so that to anyone of those days, the mid-century expressions 'young marrieds' and 'young mums' would appear contradictions in terms. The vernacular expression for 'my wife' and even sometimes 'my mother' was, at the lowest level, 'my old woman'; even the expression 'the missus' had an almost prosperous sound. A mum of 30 was often harassed, bedraggled and beslippered, and forever berating the kids for 'getting under her feet' or yelling at them to stop doing something. 'I'll *learn* you, my lady,' was one of her more terrible cries. On the other hand, a mum in her mid-forties might have the roundness of girth that made Hoggart think 'of gallons of tea, hundredweights of bread and plates of fish and chips'. Some mums of this age in the wilder back-streets of London wore a man's cloth cap on their head and an apron made out of bits of old sack, and greeted the return of their husbands from the Saturday night pubs with the enraged screams of embattled Furies. Other older mums could be of the small, pinched, wiry kind, for ever in a state of trembling worry; and by the end of a long day their lined faces looked almost martyred with tiredness. None of this was surprising if one bears in mind that at best they inhabited a dingy Victorian terrace house, at the worst a back-to-back and that in London even a quite respectable working-class home might be one floor of an inadequately converted Victorian house where the family sink would be discovered by opening what had once been a bedroom cupboard, where the wc would be two flights down and the bathroom non-existent. Babies' napkins would not, in such conditions, be washed; they would be hung to dry over a fire-guard, filling the whole tall house with a penetrating ammoniac stink.

Tyneside interior, 1938; the family's whole stock of food is on the table

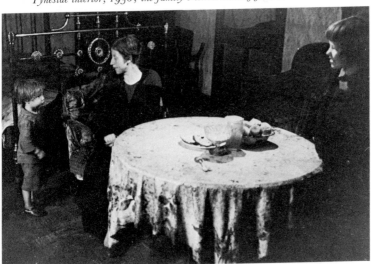

Mealtime for an unemployed London family, 1939

Even when preserved from the more searing effects of urban poverty by the boon of continuous employment (like those princes of the working class, railwaymen and postmen) or by a vitality sufficiently resistant to rheumatism and bronchitis, 'our Mum' and 'our Dad' belonged to a way of life wholly different from that of the bridge-playing shop-gazing wives of Southern Electric's season-ticket-holders. Whereas the desired feminine style of the time was an ideal compounded of fantasies and visions as old as the troubadours or as Botticelli and Raphael, or as new as Irene Forsyte, Gladys Cooper and *No, No, Nanette*, our mum had more in common with the maternity symbols of primitive non-European art. She was creator, provider and comforter. Neither husband nor sons helped with the domestic chores, for these were rituals exclusive to mum. Her only acolytes were her daughters, her only salvation in time of trouble the women from down the street or the midwife. Hence, Shaw's unusually accurate observation that home was 'the girl's prison and the mother's workhouse'. Sons were, by the standards of all other classes, cosseted and spoiled, and their upbringing almost as wholly within mum's jurisdiction as the raising of daughters, dad being invoked only in the gravest of crises. In return for her services, the most a mum could expect was an occasional cup of tea in bed. Nobody opened doors for her. Nobody said anything endearing or affectionate to her, but only about her, in her absence or post-mortem; and nobody was likely to bring her flowers in all the interval between her wedding-day and her funeral. Yet the quality of her personality might well deserve the tribute paid by the poet, George Barker, to his own mother:

> She is a procession no one can follow after
> But be like a little dog following a brass band.

Sexual pleasure had almost no part in mum's married life and little enough in courting days. When asked by earnest, progressive ladies in clinics if they enjoyed sexual intercourse, such mums would answer, 'What is there to enjoy?' It was something they had to put up with. Had D. H. Lawrence ever talked about the 'radiant pain' of sex to a mum she would have reckoned nothing to the radiance but gone on a great deal about the pain; and our dad was likely to say he preferred his glass of bitter any day. Sex meant probable pregnancy. Birth control was regarded as shudderingly unnatural, was resented by dad and, for the poorest mums, was too embarrassing to come by and too expensive to pay for. Between the wars, the only people who limited their families were those who could have afforded not to. In consequence of this and of the conditions in which they lived and worked, the domestic conversation of the working class was obsessively concerned with illness. The women dwelt so gnawingly upon the gynaecological catastrophes to which their sex was liable that to be 'eaten up with rheumatism' seemed but a minor misfortune. The men were much the same: he's gone at last, poor bugger, been ailing for months, we must think it's for the best, they think it was cancer, the doctors couldn't do nothing, a happy release. They dwelt on it all as cultured people might dwell on the tragedy of Lear or the gloomier plays of Ibsen; but, for the working class, tragedy was not something enacted on a stage by hired mimic sufferers whom one could observe or not as one pleased. It was something in which they were themselves involved and which was as inevitable as pregnancy, sickness and old age. And their queueing

Clinic room, Marie Stopes Birth Control Clinic

Daily Express *cartoonist, Strube, striking a note of good cheer in 1936. The rosy dawn of rearmament offers the unemployed hope for the future*

before curtain-rise was the day-long vigil in the vast great hospital waiting-room, culminating in such medical care as society's charity chose to spare for them.

Our dad had likewise little resemblance to the accepted image of the race, and none at all to the muscular worker with the clenched fist who strode towards the sunlight of the Revolution in the left-wing posters. He was as often as not below average height, frequently ill-shaped, and liable to sit about the house immobile, silent and shirt-sleeved, behind an outstretched newspaper. He was waited on hand and foot, and much of what has since come, with perhaps an excess of flattery, to be called his 'culture' tended to be belligerently anti-cultural. His social life was centred on the nearest pub, invariably a graceless, over-crowded place, reeking of stale beer, sweat and sour tobacco. He spoke of going 'down the pub' or 'up the Crown' and not, like his self-conscious suburbanite plagiarizers of 30 years later, of 'going to the local'. He drank nothing but beer, and nobody had yet turned dart-playing into a cult. It is conceivable, though not inevitable, that if he were a northerner he might play in a brass band; and provided he did not live in a council house, where such unhygienic activities were sometimes prohibited, he might keep pigeons or whippets. Although their greatest days were coming to an end, he might belong to one of the great Friendly Societies, such as the Rechabites or the Odd Fellows. The latter, the Manchester Unity Independent Order of Odd Fellows, was not only a prosperous and well organized insurance and benevolent club, providing, according to contributions, some of the bare rudiments of social security ahead of the Welfare State, such as sick-pay, minuscule pensions and 'distress grants'; it offered, as well, a poor man's Masonic lodge, complete with aprons, rituals, passwords, Ladies' Nights, and archaically worded 'lectures' on the virtues of Thrift, Sobriety, Benevolence and Brotherly Love. Or he might belong to the Buffaloes (the Royal Antediluvian Order of Buffaloes) which was more energetically convivial and a great organizer of outings and beanfeasts for both young and old.

The virtues of the stable working-class home were its deep interior loyalty, its immense pride in its independence and its total sincerity. Its weakness lay in its economic involvement in a system that was crumbling in the North and transforming itself in the South. Even when the system had been relatively

stable, sickness, even mere temporary unemployment, and the onset of old age could be like fatal wounds. Now that the old system was falling apart, they counted themselves lucky indeed if they did not fall down with it.

The plight of those who were permanently unemployed or only intermittently in work was

Untypical scene in a typical pub. An adventurous 'padre' plays dominoes with a group of 'regulars'

Men at the Dogs: Greyhound Racing at White City Stadium, London, 1927

likely to be dire. In 1934 the BBC broadcast a series of talks by
unemployed men and women entitled 'Time to Spare'. It was introduced by S. P. B. Mais, a popular writer of travel books and,
to guarantee its respectability, the series was summed up by a
clergyman. Since the BBC was required not to be controversial,
the scripts of the talks were certain to contain nothing inflamma-
tory; indeed one unemployed man protested against the vetting
of his script and did not broadcast at all. The published record of
the talks is, therefore, the more painful as providing evidence of
how much misery could be revealed to the general public without it being considered likely seriously to disturb them. The wife
of a ship's riveter on Clydeside reported that in 12½ years he had
had only one year's work. They had had no holiday for 13 years.
He had never been to a football match. He made cups for the
children out of condensed-milk tins, and patches for the kettle (it
had six) out of cocoa tins. They had five children. It was 'an
expense' to practise birth control (though the doctor's fee for
attending a confinement was given as two guineas and the midwife's as 25*s*.). They lived in three rooms, had no sink, and all
water was carried up and down two flights. The unemployment
pay for this family of seven was 33*s*. Their main diet was bread
and margarine and tea, the total amount of money spent on
food for the whole family each week being 16*s*.

Another contributor had had four years' work out of the previous 11. His family of four had unemployment pay of 27s. 3d. Rent took 11s., and after other expenses they had 8s. a week for food, of which 3s. went on bread. Their other purchases were three tins of skimmed milk, 4 lb. of sugar and 1½ lb. of margarine. A third contributor's family had meat (four-pennyworth of stewing beef) only on Friday, the day the dole was drawn; Sunday dinner consisted solely of potatoes. A fourth speaker, who had had 11 days' work in eight years, noted that when they went out, members of unemployed families borrowed one another's boots and overcoats and underclothes. An out-of-work clerk declared that he had been given notice while on holiday by a firm which had employed him for 16 years. It was not their practice to give testimonials. Out of his earnings of 75s. he had had mortgage payments of 25s. His unemployment insurance pay was just enough to cover his mortgage payments; for the rest he was now living on his savings. 'Even if I get back to work it will be years before I catch up again,' he said, adding what was perhaps the most significant sentence of all, 'Nothing that I could have done could have prevented it.'

Many relatively unskilled workers who were in irregular employment were little better off. One of the many casework reports of the thirties contains the story of the wife of a fitter's

The Daily Mirror *reported on 29 November 1932 that these unemployed men were paid at the rate of six shillings a ton for collecting pebbles on Sheringham Beach, Norfolk*

mate living in Bermondsey in east London. Even when he was in work, of the 43*s.* she had for housekeeping, barely 25*s.* were available for food and fuel for a household that contained three children. Most family budgets at this level, whether of the unemployed or of the intermittently employed suggest that the average weekly expenditure on food was something between 2*s.* 6*d.* and 3*s.* a head. The calculation was that the 'average' weekly amount per head spent on food in the thirties was just under 9*s.*, though in 1933 the British Medical Association satisfied itself, but hardly anybody else, that an average man could be adequately supplied with calories (though not with foods he would want to eat) for 5*s.* 11*d.* A Yorkshirewoman living in a council house, with eight children and a husband who had been two years without work, gave her own daily diet as, tea for breakfast, bread and lard or margarine for dinner (because after serving nine people with stew and potatoes she couldn't face eating any for herself), bread and butter with tinned tomatoes and black pudding at tea-time and (but only three times a week) a one-sixth share of a supper-time meal consisting of threepennyworth of chips and a pennyworth of fried fish. In general, fish and chips was probably the most wholesome food these people ever ate—when they could afford it; tea, tinned milk, margarine, bread and potatoes seem to have been their staple diet.

As might be expected, the unemployed and the unskilled were the most ill-housed unless they were lucky enough to have a council house. Many of them tried to bring up large families of young children in two rooms without running water, water closet, pantry, copper or cooking stove, on an upper floor of an old-fashioned house originally built for one-family occupation in the 1860s. In towns such as Wigan, Barnsley and Sheffield they might inhabit back-to-back houses of two or three storeys, with only one room on each storey, all of them damp, dark and bug-ridden. Investigators found that large numbers of children in the Shoreditch area of London shared a bedroom with one or two adults, that about a third of one representative group slept four or more to a room and that the sharing of a bed by five persons, or a bedroom by ten, was not unheard of. And these phenomena, of bad living conditions, inadequate feeding and permanent or intermittent unemployment, afflicted several million people throughout the interwar period.

The cumulative effect on those who endured these circumstances was a terrible apathy. In the wives it was the product of crucifying overwork and nagging ill health; in the men it was born of despair. If the husband was at work he certainly came home to dinner and so did the children; and if the husband were out of work he still had to be fed. There was no peace at night, for there were more adults and children than there were beds, and more beds than there were rooms; and with one child barely weaned there was probably another already conceived. There were no holidays, hardly ever a day out, and rarely, for the woman, more than an hour or so's respite from six in the morning till 11 at night. For many, even a visit to the pictures was impossible. The cramped, dark and overcrowded conditions, the lack of the most elementary household facilities; the endless struggle to wash and mend a pitifully inadequate supply of clothing, or to keep clean a room too cluttered, or too damp and bug-ridden, for it ever to be possible to clean it out; the effort involved in putting on even the crudest of meals whilst coping with children some of whom at least were fundamentally unwanted, aged and exhausted these women not only physically but mentally. Middle-class social workers, well fed, decently educated and knowledgeable, were astonished at the ignorance of these women about such welfare services as existed, their lethargy about birth control, their unwillingness to believe that raw carrots were better for their children than cheap jam, their passion for hot tea laced with tinned milk and their aversion from fresh herrings, and their desperate conviction that all they could do was to struggle on day after day in the same old way without once trying to organize something better for themselves. Much of this well-intentioned desire to get these wives to take on themselves the additional burden of putting right a state of affairs that would never have happened to them in the first place had the country's affairs been properly managed, arose from a failure to realize just what an excess of vitality and what strength of character this would have required. As it was, more working-class women performed wonders for their families in such conditions than society had any right to expect.

Psychological debility was even more obvious in the men since, now that they were unemployed, they had nothing to do. They sat or stood about. When first unemployed, they persuaded themselves they were 'bound' to get another job soon; but swiftly it became obvious that the opposite was almost a certainty and thereafter they regularly went no further afield than the Labour Exchange from which they drew their unemployment pay. In some shipyard, cotton or mining towns, above all in South Wales, the desolation was almost universal. Such towns ceased to be smoke-filled or clattering and became quiet economic graveyards full of skilled men who seemed likely never to work again. At the other end of the scale were youngsters who had never worked at all, their lives given meaning only by regular packets of fags and occasional club-room games of billiards. Both types, belonging wholly as they did to communities whose only historic reason for coming into existence at all was that they were a labour force for shipyard, cotton-mill or coal-mine, lost the essential core of their personality when their labour ceased to be required. They showed

And still they wait: Wigan Labour Exchange, 1939

no disposition to revolt and little enough even to demonstrate
or march. The young ones would have earned little more in a
job than they got from the dole; the old were not actually
starving and were for the most part incapable of abandoning
their lifelong pride in that sober respectability which was as
much a skilled man's guarantee of social status as his job itself.
Here again was an apathy which fretted middle-class well-
wishers. Why did the unemployed not do more for themselves
and why, when clubs were organized for them, did not more of
them come? S. P. B. Mais, when introducing the BBC's unemployed speakers, well illustrated this unfortunate tendency to
regard the unemployed as though they were handicapped
children or refugees from some natural catastrophe. He asked
his listeners to seek out an unemployed family and then 'make
it possible for them to enjoy some of the amenities we enjoy'.
Join or start an occupational club for unemployed men, he
brightly suggested, charging them a penny a week for membership; sell them leather at the cheapest rate and let them learn
how to mend their own boots. That something constructive
should be done to get these men back to meaningful work and
to relieve their wives of their grinding drudgery was never
seriously considered. Conservatives said it would cost too much
and thus prejudice full recovery from the Depression; Socialists
tended to rest content with saying it was inevitable under
capitalism and incurable while capitalism lasted. G. D. H.
Cole, who passed as an economist as well as a Socialist, had
little to suggest other than to raise the school-leaving age, award
earlier old-age pensions and to rely on the falling birth-rate to
solve the problem eventually by continuing its decline for the
rest of the century.

Having no cure for unemployment, politicians devoted their
attention to squalid wrangles as to what sums of money it was
proper to disburse to those without work. By the mid thirties
all payments to the unemployed who had exhausted (or had
never earned) a right to unemployment insurance pay were
distributed by a nationally controlled Unemployment Assis-
tance Board, set up in 1934, and subject (from 1931 onwards)
to what was known to officials as a 'household needs test' but

to everybody else as 'the means test'. The purpose of this was to vary (i.e. usually to reduce) the amount of dole a man received, by relating it to his household's 'needs'. In practice this meant continuous official inquiry into his own and his wife's savings and expenditure, and into the incomes, if any, of his dependants. UAB officials visited the unemployed man's home to find out whether his dole should be cut because one of his children earned money on a paper round or because his working daughter had had 1s. a week rise, or to discover whether a child's sudden acquisition of a new coat was indicative of a hitherto undisclosed increase in the total family income; and all such increases were required to be reported instantly. The means test, with its humiliating invasion of domestic privacy, was by far the most explosive issue raised by the unemployment problem. Its purpose was the good, old-fashioned one of discouraging the poor from thinking they had a right to money they had not worked for and the convincingly up-to-date one of enforcing cuts in public expenditure in order not to prejudice economic recovery.

Hatred of the means test was uppermost in the minds of those who took part in the National Hunger Marches of unemployed men. In 1931, 2,500 unemployed marched to London with a petition to Parliament against the means test. They were subjected to police baton charges in Hyde Park and the petition never reached Parliament. Another such march, in 1934, though spared a clash with the police, failed to persuade the Prime Minister (it was Ramsay MacDonald) to receive a delegation. In 1936 was staged the most memorable march of all, the so-called 'Jarrow Crusade'. Jarrow's shipyard had been closed by a consortium, regardless of the town's total dependence on shipbuilding for its livelihood. The Government refused to intervene or to give rearmament contracts to the district, asserting, fatuously, that Jarrow would have to work out its own salvation. Funds were collected, helpers organized and 200 men selected to undertake the 300-mile march to the capital. They set off after an inter-denominational religious service and with the public approval of the Suffragan Bishop of Jarrow, though his approval was only temporary owing to the displeasure the

The Jarrow Marchers halt for a meal of hot corned beef and potatoes at a farm near Bedford

march caused the Bishop of Durham. They were led for the first
12 miles by the Mayor and Mayoress of Jarrow, and for most
of the rest of the way by their passionately zealous Labour MP,
Ellen Wilkinson, who, characteristically, was rebuked at the
Labour Party Conference for her irresponsibility. At Ripon a
service was held for them in the Cathedral; and at Leicester the
local Co-op mended their boots. As they approached London,
Oswald Mosley's Blackshirts rampaged through Bethnal Green.
The metropolis received the marchers with soup-kitchens and
a certain gawping incomprehension. Ellen Wilkinson presented
Jarrow's petition in the Commons and the Government
answered with perfunctory platitudes. For many MPs the whole
thing was a stunt worked up by an emotional female redhead.
The marchers went home with nothing achieved and had their
dole money cut because they had not been available for work
(not that there was any) during the period of their march. In
the end, it was left to Hitler to solve England's unemployment

problem by driving its Government to rearmament and to the conscription of the entire labour force for the prosecution of total war. The Welfare State that emerged after that war was not created out of mere sentimental humanitarianism. It was created mainly out of angry disgust at the humiliations suffered by millions of people between the wars under Governments composed of men deficient in both intelligence and imagination.

Further Reading

J. B. Priestley, *English Journey*, 1933, Chapters 4–10 and pages 406–18; *Time to Spare*, the scripts of the BBC broadcasts by unemployed men and women in 1934; Margery Spring Rice, *Working-Class Wives*, 1939; *Our Towns: A Close Up*, a survey made by the Women's Group on Public Welfare, 1943; and three books all originally published by the Left Book Club: George Orwell, *The Road to Wigan Pier*, 1937, G. D. H. Cole, *Condition of Britain*, 1937, and Ellen Wilkinson, *Jarrow, The Town That Was Murdered*, 1939. As suggested in the text, Richard Hoggart, *Uses of Literacy*, has something to say about the employed as well as the unemployed working class before 1939, especially in Chapters 1–5.

XI

The Sweet and the Sour

Nothing was more revealing of the change of mood that came over the nation in 1931 than the universal acclaim accorded in that year (and, later on, to the film version) to a patriotic musical spectacular, Noel Coward's *Cavalcade*, staged at Drury Lane. It was an event, not so much in the history of the West End stage as in the history of the British people. It told how an upper-middle-class couple, Jane and Robert, preserved their courage and dignity through a succession of public and private events, mostly distressing, ranging from the relief of Mafeking to the Armistice of 1918. But though the story ends in 1918, it is more than an exercise in nostalgia. There is a two-part epilogue. First, Jane and Robert drink together on the eve of New Year's Day, 1930. Jane says, 'Let's couple the future of England with the past of England', and after grave references to the victories, triumphs, glories and sorrows that are over, she concludes, 'And let's drink to the hope that some day this country of ours, which we love so much, will find dignity and greatness and peace again.'

But that was not enough. The way ahead must be more carefully signposted. There followed one final scene: a night-club, with a girl stridently singing 'Twentieth Century Blues'. The cacophony increases until the final stage direction: 'The lights slowly come up and the whole stage is composed of massive tiers, upon which stand the entire Company. The Union Jack flies over their heads as they sing "God Save the King".'

From the first night of *Cavalcade* onwards, the hectic twenties were as dead as Queen Anne; and a fortnight afterwards, the electorate patriotically voted the National Government into power for the whole of the thirties. It is not surprising, therefore,

George V and Queen Mary at the opening of the Mersey Tunnel, 1935. The Queen wears her invariable 'toque'

that thereafter the life of the non-political majority was stirred by only two events, both royal and both calculated to touch patriotic heart-strings. In 1935 nation-wide celebrations commemorated the Silver Jubilee of George V and Queen Mary. Public buildings were floodlit (a striking novelty). Their Majesties processed to St Paul's for a Thanksgiving Service and received Addresses from Parliament. They drove in open carriage through the London slums and were everywhere received with enthusiasm. Throughout the land, windows, streets and lamp standards were decorated with banners, bunting and flags. It was all so tumultuously affectionate that the King wrote, 'The greatest number of people in the streets that I have ever seen in my life', and was reported to have said, 'I am beginning to think they must like me for myself'. They almost certainly did. He looked exactly the kind of father-figure the people of the thirties imagined their grandparents had looked up to—a kind-hearted, gruff-voiced village squire, or one of those small master-businessmen Baldwin had idealized, with simple dignity, sound common sense and no truck whatever with newfangled ideas and dubious modern manners. And there by his side, asserting more visibly still the enduringness of old ways and values, was Queen Mary. Always, she wore a dignified pre-1914 kind of hat called a 'toque'. She had a regal bosom and her skirts had a down-to-the-ground length that other women in the land had abandoned a decade earlier. She was Lady of the Manor to a whole people; as indefatigable in the public duties of her position as the King was in his, and perhaps at a greater personal cost, since she was a woman of some taste married to a rather peppery philistine. No two people

184

thought or behaved less like the more intelligent, adventurous and progressive-minded people in England than the King and the Queen; yet no king and consort had ever earned and kept so much affection and respect.

Eight months later, in January 1936, the King died, his approaching end being announced with the words, 'The King's life is moving peacefully towards its close'. His successor, Edward VIII, was regarded as go-ahead and somewhat devil-may-care. As Prince of Wales he had saved the Royal Family from appearing completely

Jubilee Tea Party, 1935

outdated by occasionally dancing at night-clubs, once breaking his collar-bone while steeplechasing, wearing the more relaxed male dress of the time and travelling over the Empire, displaying smiling diffidence, youthful gaiety and an attractive impression of being slightly apologetic about the whole business of being royal. But within a few months of his accession, it came to light that he proposed to marry a Mrs Wallis Simpson, an American who had already divorced one husband and was in process of divorcing a second. The British, but not the foreign, Press had printed nothing about the King's association with Mrs Simpson; but began to do so when on 1 December 1936 the Bishop of Bradford preached a sermon in which he said the King ought to go to church more often. The leading articles were for the most part solemnly disapproving and full of ponderous references to a Grave Constitutional Crisis. By then Baldwin had already made it clear to the

Edward VIII broadcasting

King that if he married Mrs Simpson he would have to abdicate. When Edward tried to keep both his throne and Mrs Simpson by proposing that she become his wife but not queen, Baldwin vetoed that too. Neither the British nor the Dominion Cabinets would pass the required legislation. Edward was firmly and speedily directed towards abdication. The appropriate Act of Parliament was pushed through all its stages between mid morning and tea-time in a single day, 11 December 1936. Before leaving the country that night, with the title of Duke of Windsor, Edward was allowed a farewell broadcast. He could not, he said, discharge his duties as King 'without the help and support of the woman I love'.

There was a brief splutter of support for Edward just before the end; but Churchill, who was tactless enough to oppose abdication in the Commons, was shouted down. Once again, Baldwin had interpreted the English mind correctly. Divorces were being made absolute in their thousands every year; but the millions continued to disapprove. For the last time, Baldwin handled a potentially divisive issue with healing words. He indulged in no moral tub-thumping; that he left to the Archbishop of Canterbury and the Editor of *The Times*. Without a public murmur of

An English Eccentric: a lone protester claims to prefer Edward VIII to Baldwin and creates bewilderment

self-congratulation or one vindictive utterance, he had contrived to present Edward as one who had put private affection before public duty, who had treated divorce as a matter of no importance, who imagined that the values of the past no longer counted, and who had caused infinite pain to his beloved and widowed mother, Queen Mary. Edward had added to his indiscretions during a visit to South Wales shortly before the crisis. Shocked by the conditions of the unemployed coal-miners, he had said, 'Something must be done.' This marked him as irresponsible, no less than did his twentyish failure to remember that, the lyrics of their popular songs notwithstanding, the English people believed that to behave as if Love Were All was the prerogative, not of kings, but only of film stars.

The throne passed to his brother, Albert, Duke of York, who immediately symbolized the re-establishment of tradition by being styled George VI. A shy man, with an impediment in his speech, he had burst into tears when he realized what was to happen to him, but he and his consort, Queen Elizabeth, more than fulfilled Queen Mary's prophecy, 'The Yorks will do it very well'. George VI had two small daughters, and already the populace was fully habituated to sentimentalisms about the 'Little Princesses'. News items such as 'Princess Margaret has

George VI and Queen Elizabeth with the Roosevelts at Hyde Park, N.Y., June 1939. The President's mother in the centre

hitherto worn only white, but now when she plays on the floor a pink linen crawler is pulled over her cambric morning frock' had been thought worthy of heavy print in the popular Press. The spectacle of what was (in the absence of a male heir for the reigning sovereign to quarrel with in the normal Hanoverian tradition) perhaps the first genuinely happy family to occupy Buckingham Palace since it had become a royal residence was immensely reassuring. 'The Yorks' were the nice, unaffected family couple that all the young marrieds of the brighter suburbs themselves aspired to be. And indeed, as in one more bout of junketing, they celebrated the Coronation of George VI and Queen Elizabeth in 1937, the English had much to congratulate themselves on. They had survived the war, its hectic aftermath, the spectre of Bolshevism, the General Strike, the threat of ruin in 1931 and the worst of the Depression. To have done so with their national unity strengthened, their political liberties intact and their traditional ideas assuringly conserved, and with signs of ever-increasing prosperity in every street except the mean streets they kept away from, was a remarkable achievement. For those who had regular work and a steady income, the thirties were serene years.

But it was an achievement that could be admired only by ignoring the contrasting poverty that survived so odiously alongside it and by a cosily insular disregard of the looming threat of European war. And so, while the many congregated together to enjoy royal occasions, the few huddled into smaller congregations and ideological sects, almost all of them prophesying doom. While the twenties were years of individualism and of experiments bright with hope, the thirties were crowded with Clubs, Groups, Unions, Fronts, Leagues and Action Committees all issuing insistent Calls—to Struggle (for Power); to Resist (Fascism); to Pledge (oneself against War); to Fight (for Freedom); to Overthrow (Capitalism); to Save (Republican Spain); to Defend (Democracy); to Declare (Solidarity with the Workers); to Plan (the economy); to Cement (the alliance between the democracies of the West and the Toiling Masses of the USSR); and to Stop (Hitler and War); and up and down the country, at mass demonstrations and in small basement rooms, impassioned speakers regularly informed their audiences that the hands of the clock were pointing to five minutes to midnight.

Most of these calls to action were the incoherent responses of men who, though more generous, more sincere and more intellectual than the mass of ordinary men or the mediocre politicians of the time, were even more susceptible to the illusory and the impracticable. Perhaps never before had serious-minded English people read, written and talked so much, felt so deeply and been so wrong about the world, and in such various ways, as they were between the wars. Almost to the end, some of them had the illusion that peace could be painlessly assured if only the Government would 'support' the League of Nations ('Do you believe in the League of Nations?' people would ask, rather as if it were the Nicene Creed); wars could be prevented if arms were made by the State instead of by those 'Merchants of Death', the armaments manufacturers; or if, instead of having armaments at all, the Government 'sincerely' advocated a system of 'collective security', even though, as early as the Japanese invasion of Manchuria in 1931, no Great Power was willing to be collected into such a system. There was the pacifist illusion that if Englishmen pledged themselves against war the whole world would do likewise in stunned admiration of England's shining moral example. There was the illusion that wars had economic causes, and that peace could be promoted if the 'satisfied' Colonial Powers 'equitably' shared their colonies with the 'have-not' countries, Germany, Italy and Japan.

Illusions about Soviet Russia abounded. It was the Fatherland of the International Proletariat; it demonstrated the virtues of State Planning; it was the only true democracy; it was 'the most Christian country in the world'; nothing but the obstinate obscurantism of those lackeys of capitalism, the National Government, prevented the Soviets from instantly giving their all to a great People's Crusade that would crush the Fascists for ever. In the same illusory fashion, Communist Parties outside the USSR, instead of being seen for what they were, mere extraterritorial agents of Soviet foreign policy, were looked on as the spearhead of a great Popular Front of all who desired to

189

Anti-Fascist Salute: British volunteer members of the International Brigade that fought for Republican Spain against General Franco give the clenched-fist workers' salute on returning to London, 1937

make common cause with the workers in the fight for Democracy. Some were so drugged by this fantasy that they called one another 'Comrade' and talked so glibly about 'the workers' that it was an effort to recall that the only workers with whom they had had dealings were probably the college servants they had tipped at Oxbridge. It was not until they learned that Hitler and Stalin had become allies in August 1939 that they realized that there is no fool like an intellectual fool. Left-wing writers had to unsay in the forties and fifties much of what they had said in the thirties; just as the innumerable advocates of agreement with Hitler in the thirties had to be particularly fierce thereafter about how wicked he had been. Finally, there was the strongly held illusion that the Spanish Civil War was an incident in the great world struggle between Fascism and Democracy and not, as it essentially was, a struggle to the death between Spaniards about Spain, and about nowhere and nobody else. The intense passion with which many Englishmen supported Republican Spain (some with their lives, as members of the International Brigade) and the equal intensity with which others saw Franco as the saviour of religion and civilization made the demonstrations elicited 30 years later by the war in Vietnam seem mere isolated public brawls.

Those spared these illusions, harboured others: Mussolini was a great statesman, cast in truly Roman mould, who shaped Fascist Italy into a State outstanding for efficiency and economic progress; in 1935 his navy was too powerful to be challenged by the British fleet, but his army too weak to conquer Abyssinia; if placated and courted, he would gratefully refrain from allying with Hitler. About Germany, the illusions were uncountable. Germany had not 'really' started the war of 1914; Germany had been 'crushed' by the Versailles Treaty, which was in all respects vengeful and unjust; the Weimar Republic had been dominated by degenerate homosexuals and had been predestined to fail; Hitler was to be applauded for making Germany a solid bulwark against Bolshevism; Hitler believed in self-determination; the Sudetenland area of Czechoslovakia had been 'taken from Germany' in 1919 and was 'returned' to it at Munich in 1938; agreements signed to promote peace under the auspices of the League of Nations in the twenties were so much worthless paper, but agreements of a like nature signed by Hitler would be kept; and if treated like a normal politician, Hitler would become one.

The most long-lasting and generally accepted illusions were those that exaggerated England's power in the world. The removal from the international scene after 1919 of the USA and the USSR, the disappearance of the Austrian and Turkish Empires and the elimination of the German fleet seemed to create, side by side with the harrowing recollections of the long casualty lists of 1914–18, the view among all classes that 'we' had won the war almost unaided and had acquired the capacity not only to defend and maintain the Empire but also to determine the success or failure of the League of Nations and to assume responsibility for the safety of the whole of Europe, Africa and Asia, all without the expense and inconvenience of either great armaments or conscription. Extremes met in this: pacifists believing in the efficacy of unilateral disarmament, internationalists demanding the use of British forces to expel Covenant-breaking Japan from Manchuria, intellectuals demanding that the British Government somehow stop Hitler persecuting Jews, and Churchill urging the British Lion to defend freedom and independence both for itself and all Europe while, of course, denying these things to Indians. Behind most of these assumptions of omnipotence lay both a forgetfulness of the parts played in the war against the Kaiser's Germany by Russia and the United States and an unquestioned belief that France was still a great military Power fully capable, if war came, of dealing punishingly with any German offensive. This universal over-valuation of England's material power in the world explains much of the sense of outrage engendered in politically conscious circles by the victories of Japan in the Far East and of Mussolini in Abyssinia and by the ease with which Hitler rearmed Germany from 1935 onwards, reoccupied the Rhineland in 1936 and annexed Austria in 1938, all in defiance of the Treaty of Versailles; by the inability of the British Government to stop the flow of men and materials from Italy and Germany to Franco from 1936 to 1939; and by the bombing of open towns from Shanghai to Guernica and Madrid.

This was not merely patriotic petulance, however. There was a wholly creditable sense of outrage among knowledgeable people of all sorts at the astonishing spectacle, almost everywhere in Europe, of the systematic destruction of political, intellectual and personal freedoms, combined with a persecution of Jews and a brutal contempt for all those rational and humane values which civilized Europe had come to take for granted since at least the end of the eighteenth century. It was this sense that something terrible was happening in Europe in the thirties, and that it would soon (in some way or other) happen in England too, that explains the melodramatic postures of fear and defiance and the increasing forecasts of catastrophe of the time. It also explains and indeed justifies the involvement of the intellectuals in left-wing politics since the especial victims of the Nazi terror were poets, writers, journalists, artists, scientists, liberals, pacifists and internationalists. If, in England, the spectacle of literary young men fresh from the public schools

192

and the older universities proclaiming their solidarity with the 'workers' was always slightly grotesque it was still a fact that, under Hitler, professors and philosophers were hunted down equally with trade unionists and social democratic politicians. The Nazis were always principally at war with the human mind; but in England, only the intellectuals, awkwardly reciting the slogans of proletarian struggle or solemnly mugging up 'the Marxist-Leninist classics' ever said so. The politicians mostly came back from Germany claiming that Hitler was gentlemanly, moderate, trustworthy and sincere, and filled with a genuine desire for peace. The highbrow anti-Fascists of the thirties failed to affect the policy of the British Government or to influence public opinion at large; and they were as blind to the evils of Stalinism as they were alert to the evils of Hitler; but they deserve a more honourable place in the record than the mass that did not listen to them and the National Government, which flattered and encouraged Hitler and Mussolini almost to the end.

It was their well-founded fear that they were getting nowhere at all that explains why the anti-Government propaganda of the thirties was so nearly hysterical. Every other message from Gollancz to the faithful of the Left Book Club was labelled TERRIBLY URGENT. 'The situation', wrote Orwell in 1937, 'is desperate.' For W. H. Auden it was so desperate that private desires must be wholly suspended: 'Tomorrow the rediscovery of romantic love . . . BUT TODAY THE STRUGGLE.' Even Churchill added his quota. In 1934 he announced that the opening hours of the next war would be accompanied by 'the crash of bombs exploding on London and cataracts of masonry, fire and smoke'.

When men began to ask themselves (though not in large numbers until 1940) why, given the axiomatic might of England, nothing was being done about these fearful dangers, the answer seemed to be clear: it was all the fault of the old and silly politicians. There can be no doubt that the political leaders of the time were unusually hostile to intelligence and ability. The most spectacular example of the frustration of energy and talent was provided by the disastrous career of Sir Oswald

Mosley. His wealth, his marriage to the daughter of the imperious Marquess Curzon, his youth (he became an MP in 1918 at the age of 20) and his ability, all clearly marked him for high office in the Conservative Party. Contemptuous of the Tories of the 1918 Parliament, he turned to Labour, won Smethwick for the Party in 1926, and in 1929 was a member of MacDonald's second Labour Government. His skill in Parliamentary debate, his power of oratory on a public platform, his fashionable good looks, which would have made him a box-office draw as a cinema hero, his personal magnetism and the fertility of his ideas, all stamped him by now as a future Labour Prime Minister. MacDonald made him one of a committee of three with special responsibility for unemployment. He produced a programme. It was sensible, constructive and imaginative. His elders and betters turned it down. He resigned in protest. He made impressive speeches to the Parliamentary Party and to Labour's annual conference. Party loyalty was too strong for him; his impatient, autocratic temperament, his flair and his style were as unacceptable to the old men of Labour as the mercurial brilliance of Lloyd George and the impulsive energy

Fascist Salute: Sir Oswald Mosley is greeted, Hitler-style, by his Blackshirt supporters in London, 1936

of Churchill were to the Conservatives. Mosley was soon to be squandering his talents in the barren follies of organizing the British Union of Fascists. The career of Oswald Mosley, like the careers during this period of Lloyd George, Churchill, the economist J. M. Keynes, and the expert on tank warfare, Liddell Hart, all of whom were also largely ignored, demonstrates that from 1922 to 1939 England's affairs were managed in accordance with Baldwin's view that the country was best served by men of second-class brains, on the grounds that men with first-class brains had second-class characters.

After the crisis of 1931 matters worsened. The Liberal Party virtually disappeared, and the Labour Party, led by Attlee from 1935, combined lack of discernible policy with a determination to expel any of its members who sought to give it one. Even the Conservative Party, for all its numerical strength, lay anaesthetized under Baldwin's smothering influence until 1937 and willingly connived thereafter at the establishment by Neville Chamberlain of what was virtually a personal dictatorship, excluding from office most of the Party's best men; so that by 1938 Churchill, Eden, Duff Cooper, Macmillan and Amery, though all Conservative MPs, were as much of a frustrated Opposition as the Labour Party. The leading members of the National Government excited quite exceptional hostility among their opponents. The meandering MacDonald gave place to the bumbling Baldwin, and he in turn to the obstinate self-immolated Chamberlain. Around them were such figures as the cheerily self-satisfied Kingsley Wood, the sparsely endowed Sir Thomas Inskip, who was made Minister of Defence to the amazement of all, and a succession of prim, pedantic and platitudinous Foreign Secretaries in Sir John Simon, Sir Samuel Hoare and Lord Halifax. It is hardly surprising that, in such company, Eden, during his brief frustrated term at the Foreign Office, should have seemed (at 40) both young and courageous. It soon became an article of faith that these men were the most foolish and incompetent ever to hold Government office since the days when Lord North had lost the American colonies.

The dispassionate historian may well consider that this meant that the National Government suffered from hardly any of the miscellaneous illusions of the time save the equally fatal one that if Hitler and Mussolini were handled calmly and gently ('appeased') they would become tame and inactive bourgeois politicians like John Simon and Tom Inskip. To contemporaries the record looked consistently feeble and humiliating. Simon had done nothing to stop the Japanese when they invaded Manchuria in 1931; Baldwin had allegedly failed to rearm the country to meet the menace of the allegedly enormous *Luftwaffe*; in 1935 Hoare had signed an agreement with the Germans, allowing them to build battleships, and another with the French planning to let Mussolini have more of Abyssinia than his armies had then conquered. Under Chamberlain there were legalistically infuriating refusals to supply arms to Republican Spain, and agreements with Mussolini by which he promised to stop supplying Franco, but all of which he broke. When Austria was swallowed up by Hitler, Chamberlain deplored Hitler's method but not his objective. When, in 1938, Hitler appeared to insist on war unless he could acquire the Sudetenland from Czechoslovakia, Chamberlain flew to Munich to ensure that Hitler got what he wanted without the trouble of going to war. When Chamberlain returned from Munich brandishing a document in which Hitler had promised to negotiate on all future disputes,

Evening Standard *cartoonist, Low, sees Chamberlain, as well as Peace and Reason, as Hitler's victims in the diplomatic struggle over Czechoslovakia in 1938*

"MEIN KAMPF"

Appeasement in progress: Neville Chamberlain with umbrella and Lord Halifax (Foreign Secretary) in Rome with Mussolini, right, January 1939. After the visitors had gone, Mussolini said, 'These men . . . are the tired sons of a long line of rich forefathers and they will lose their Empire'

the nation showed its mind by cheering him ecstatically for having at the eleventh hour released them from the fear of war and by revealing, via the opinion polls a few weeks later, that they did not think Hitler's word could be trusted.

Munich probably made it certain that, if war threatened again, Chamberlain would be forced by Parliamentary pressure to oppose him and that the public would acquiesce in that pressure. One Munich was enough. And so, over Poland in 1939, Chamberlain had nothing with which to counter yet another threat of force from Hitler save a threat to use force in return. It was an empty threat since, with the Soviet Union allying with Hitler in August and the French determined to do no more than stay put behind the Maginot Line, Chamberlain could not save the Poles; he had no force to save them with. The last English illusions of the time were the illusions of the last months of 1939: the illusion that 'time was on our side' and that Hitler could be beaten in the end by economic blockade; and

The end of Civvy Street: the smiles do not altogether hide the apprehension

the illusion that, having failed altogether to save Poland from Hitler, England could somehow save Finland from Stalin.

And so, to an extent that, as their perspectives lengthen and their analysis deepens, historians may fail to understand, the English ended the years of peace with an extraordinary sense of guilt. Through failure to be resolute, though indifference and self-indulgence and above all because of their tame devotion to a Government composed of old and silly men, they had caused, in Churchill's phrase, 'an unnecessary war'. The Chinese, the Abyssinians, the persecuted Jews, the exiled and imprisoned scientists and intellectuals of central Europe, the people of Guernica, the martyred Czechs and, at home, the starving families on the dole and in the slums, were all on the national conscience because of the failures and shames of what was henceforth to be labelled, in W. H. Auden's words, 'a mean and sordid decade'.

In January 1940 Louis MacNiece contributed the following poem to the *New Statesman*. It was called *Interregnum*:

> *Twenty years forgetting*
> *Twenty years turning the Nelson eye*
> *Our wings heavy with the pollen*
> *Of flowers about to die*
> *We said, 'Make merry in the sunshine',*
> *At least we are alive.*
> *But now the sun has set behind the hangar*
> *There is no honey in the hive.*

History is unlikely long to consider this as an accurate verdict on the years between the wars. But, as someone once wrote, 'Legends live longer than history because, perhaps, they are truer than history.'

Further Reading

Seaman, *op. cit.*, pages 247–316, has a critical analysis of the National Government's foreign policy and of the left-wing opposition to it. Mowat, *op. cit.*, though good on the latter, is a little outdated on the former. Taylor, *op. cit.*, pages 346–452, treats the thirties as altogether a case of much ado about not a great deal, and Malcolm Muggeridge's coruscating *The Thirties*, 1940, from which Mr Taylor got one or two of his jokes, makes the whole decade appear much funnier than it actually was to live through.

INDEX

The numbers in **heavy type** refer to pages on which illustrations appear

Wales, Prince of, 67
Wallace, Edgar, 119
Wallace, Nellie, 94
Wall's Ice Cream, **156**
Waste Land, The, 22
Waugh, Alec, 109
Waugh, Evelyn, 68
Webb, Beatrice, 39–41, 81–2
Well of Loneliness, The, 59
Wells, H. G., 116, 117
Wembley Stadium, 160–**1**, 163
West Bromwich, 166
West, Mae, 46
Wheatley, John, 29
White City Stadium, **174**
Whiteman, Paul, 89
Wigan, coal strike 1921, **35**; unemployment 1930s, 176, **178**

Wilkinson, Ellen, 119, 181
Wilson, President Woodrow, 16
Winn, Godfrey, 120
Winterton, Lord, 37
Wireless, *see* Broadcasting

Wodehouse, P. G., 64, 115, 119–20
Woman magazine, **121**
Women, changing social status of, 52–4, 63; fashions, 54–8, **58**, **61**, 62–3, **64**; clubs, **57**; magazines, 120–2; employment of, 53–4; and birth control, 58–9, 63; working class, 63
Women's League of Health and Beauty, 163
Woolworth's, **49**, 94, 117, 156
Working class, after 1939, 166–71; men, 172–3; women, 168–71; housing, 169, 176–7; health, 170, 171–2; songs, 96–7; diet, 175, 176
Wythenshawe, 148, **149**

Yates, Dornford, 18
'Yes We Have No Bananas', nonsense song of 1923, **89**
Young Woodley, 59
Youth Hostel Movement, 163

Zinoviev Letter, **30**, 31